THE HOLLYWOOD BODY METHOD

THE HOLLYWOOD BODY METHOD

Practical Steps for a Sustainable, Healthy Lifestyle to Look Younger and Feel Your Best

Irina Cazazaeva

Published by Game Changer Publishing

Paperback ISBN: 978-1-967424-31-3

Hardcover ISBN: 978-1-967424-32-0

Digital ISBN: 978-1-967424-33-7

www.GameChangerPublishing.com

DEDICATION

To Sasha and Anna.
Thank you for showing how unconditional love feels.

READ THIS FIRST

Just to say thanks for buying and reading my book, I would like to give you some bonus resources, no strings attached!

Scan the QR Code Here:

THE HOLLYWOOD BODY METHOD

PRACTICAL STEPS FOR A SUSTAINABLE, HEALTHY LIFESTYLE TO LOOK YOUNGER AND FEEL YOUR BEST

IRINA CAZAZAEVA

ACKNOWLEDGMENTS

"I first met Irina in 2006 when I was a member of the Producing team on a Warner Bros film in Montreal. I was immediately impressed with her fluency in five languages, her attention to detail, and her work ethic. At that time she was already laying the groundwork to launch what would become a successful international nutrition and fitness consultancy.

We've stayed in touch ever since, and I was happy to reconnect with her a couple of years ago on another project. When she shared her nutritional and fitness outline, I was so impressed by her flexible approach to diet and fitness that I hired her to coach our actors on that show, and the following ones. Her fitness regime is not a one-size-fits-all approach. Each person received a unique personalized portfolio to guide them on their successful health journey with great results. So much so that they continued to follow Irina's plan after the projects wrapped. Irina will be my first call on each and every project going forward to help the actors achieve total health.

I highly recommend Irina's Sustainable Lifestyle Plan to anyone wishing to improve the quality of their life."

– Mark McNair, film producer

"Irina is the absolute best! I not only have been feeling great, but my performance with the trainer has been getting better."

– Michael Iskander, actor

"Irina is incredibly kind and compassionate. Her thoughtful approach to wellness and coaching helped me through a difficult film shoot for nine months. Irina is a pillar of strength and a light."

– Haley Bennett, actor

"From the moment I met Irina, it was clear that her passion for health and well-being isn't just a career—it's a way of life. Her genuine kindness, unwavering dedication, and natural ability to inspire others shine through in everything she does, making her not only an expert in nutrition but also a true advocate for living a balanced and joyful life."

– Marie-Françoise Pereira

"I've been feeling really good. The weight drop has been nice and even. Muscle definition is looking good."

–Avan Jogia, actor

"My journey with Irina started about 4 years ago, and like so many others, I was primarily concerned with extra weight and the way it impacted my looks. However, Irina's guidance went far beyond mere numbers on a scale. She became my guide to discovering how to feel truly healthy and vibrant. Irina coached me during my pregnancy and postpartum, and it is because of her expert guidance that I feel energetic, healthy, youthful, and once again love the reflection I see in the mirror—just as I did two decades ago."

– Anna Aronova from www.aronova.nyc

"*Working with Irina Cazazaeva is a truly transformative journey—one of growth, discovery, and empowerment. I am not only changing my body composition and losing weight, but I am also deepening my connection with my mind, body, and spirit. Through her unique alchemy of science, nutrition, and mindset work, she creates a highly effective yet deeply personalized approach. Her guidance goes beyond just the physical—she nurtures my whole essence, helping me step into my most empowered, most aligned self. Most importantly, she is teaching me to embrace and celebrate the journey itself—to find joy in the process of learning, growing, and evolving—with her wisdom, encouragement, and unwavering belief in my potential, I am experiencing lasting change in multiple aspects of my life, becoming my truest and most fulfilled self.*"

– With love and gratitude, Leslie Bishop

"*Irina is wonderful, positive, showing great compassion and care for the person wanting to lose weight; she is focused on helping achieve a sustainable healthy lifestyle. Irina is extremely supportive and encourages you every step of the way. I feel very blessed to have her alongside me as I work toward my goal. It is a privilege to be part of this program.*"

– Claudette Brault from www.claudette-brault-montreal-artist.com

CONTENTS

INTRODUCTION
DITCH DIETING TO BUILD A LOW-EFFORT, LASTING HEALTHY LIFESTYLE

Desperation is the raw material of drastic change.
Only those who can leave behind everything they
have ever believed in can hope to escape.
– William S. Burroughs, *The Western Lands*

Hi! I am Irina, a registered holistic nutritionist, mindset coach, Theta healer, and naturopath. I'm also a mother, wife, sister, aunt, friend. I wrote this book for several reasons, one of them being to support my clients as they embark on their journey to optimal well-being and longevity. In it, I share simple steps to help you create a low-effort, healthy lifestyle strategy, stick to your plan consistently, and avoid harming your health through dieting or getting trapped in a yo-yo cycle.

As I write these words, my daughter has just turned 12. I started dieting at 14, and this is the book I wish I had read when I was searching for ways to maximize my performance at school, stay fit, and feel more confident.

And this book is for you, my friend—to motivate you to change bad habits, stick to healthy routines, overcome self-sabotage, and become the best version of yourself. The world needs the best version of you.

How do I know that you are wonderful, even though you might feel like the worst piece of crap right now? Because at the lowest point in my life, I felt like the only thing I deserved was to die as quickly as possible before I broke my own heart once again with another unfulfilled promise to clean up my act and start living a better life.

Over 15 years ago, I backed myself into a corner by slowly giving in to bad habits—overeating, overindulging, self-medicating with drugs and alcohol, and using all kinds of quick fixes society offers to escape reality while pretending, *I'm fine!*

On the outside, I presented myself as a well-spoken, outgoing, fun-loving, hard-working rebel with all kinds of causes. On the inside, I felt broken. I didn't even want to confront my trauma and other issues because, in my mind, I was supposed to die young. I carried a big black hole in my stomach that I tried to fill with pasta, shoes, dresses, parties, and more. That black hole fed on pure negativity, sometimes disguised as self-care, self-pity, or demands for my fair share of love and excitement.

Every time I gave in and fed it, it demanded more—more chaos, more broken promises and hearts, more anger, resentment, shame, self-pity, and indulgence. I was diagnosed with eating disorders and depression and cycled from one addiction to another: overeating, obsessing over what to eat, exercising, falling in love, working, making money, spending money, drugs, alcohol—then working more, spending more, and using more drugs and alcohol.

Then came the moment when the black hole took over. I could no longer control my self-medication with drugs and alcohol. But I was smacked with the most unexpected gift—desperation. When I had tried *everything* and *nothing worked*, I finally asked for help and, to my astonishment, I received plenty.

Help came in the form of a self-help group filled with strangers eager to hug me and tell me they loved me and wanted me to come back. And my gurus: Richard O'Connor, Eckhart Tolle, Esther and Jerry Hicks, Marianne Williamson, Julia Cameron, Napoleon Hill, Bob Proctor, Hina Khan, and others.

At first, I stopped hurting. Then, I started feeling like I belonged among the living and that I could be healed. One day at a time, my depression lifted. I was able to control my compulsive behavior, and the black hole disappeared. I felt serene, happy, and trusted my path.

In trying to answer my own questions, I studied naturopathy, nutrition, epigenetics, and neuroscience, developing a set of daily habits that help me live my best life in the healthiest body I've ever had—waking up with enthusiasm, enjoying my family life, and working with purpose. I started sharing my experiences in overcoming my struggles with others and became a nutrition, longevity, and mindset coach.

I began working as a nutritionist with Hollywood actors and created my own body-transformation formula, which I call the Hollywood Body Method. The method is based on actor preparation techniques—changing the body from the inside out, beginning with a goal that ignites you, then designing a new self-image you admire, discarding old layers of sabotage, living your life from this new self-image, and falling in love with your new self. Any external change without internal mindset work is a sad waste of time and effort.

Here's what I envision for you: if you keep an open mind, allow this book to inspire you, and use the simple tips to replace bad habits that keep you stuck with a new, healthy routine, you, too, can feel invigorated and achieve optimal health—without it feeling like a chore.

Whatever you do, don't let diet culture suck you in. Don't judge your body based on current beauty standards, and don't give a flying saucer what others think about the way you look.

But do take care of your body, mind, and spirit. Truly make an effort to feel healthy and happy every day. Let your well-being be your top priority in a sustainable way—because your life depends on it. Seriously, it does. Our life here on Earth begins and ends with the body.

One thing you can be certain of is that your life will end. I've seen people die. You probably have, too. So let's stop pretending that we'll live forever and have all the time in the world to enjoy life. How you care for your body and what you do with your life between now and your last breath matters.

Numerous research studies conclude that the foundation of your health lies in your **eating** and **lifestyle habits**. Things like sleeping too little, consuming too much sugar, drinking alcohol, enduring chronic stress, and allowing insufficient time for love and connection all influence your gene expression, lowering your natural health potential. Thus, we can safely conclude that your life depends on the quality of your lifestyle.

Many of the lifestyle habits you've developed are deeply embedded in your subconscious mind. You absorbed them from your family, caregivers, and the people around you during early childhood —when your subconscious was open to receiving information as absolute truth.

The good news? *You* are still in control. You can erase outdated habits and develop new ones that sustain your health and energy.

The way you eat affects the production of neurotransmitters and hormones, which determine how you handle stress. If you're unhappy with how you look, you might subconsciously hide at work. And even if you're the perfect candidate for the next promotion, it may go to your colleague who puts herself out there with confidence. If you've forgotten how great exercise feels because [insert your favorite excuse here], deep down, you may sense that something is missing. That feeling of unease spreads to those around you, creating a ripple effect: something's missing… something's missing…

This book is a reminder that you are divine perfection. There is nothing wrong with you. If you're searching for a new way to feel your best, all you have to do is peel away the layers of what no longer serves you, create a low-effort, healthy lifestyle you enjoy, and sustain it every day. Amen.

So, what should you do if you've noticed you've gained weight and your favorite clothes feel too tight?

Let me sprinkle in some holistic nutritionist wisdom: weight gain is a complex interplay of genetics, hormones, diet, and lifestyle. May you find the strength to resist diet culture and its standardized, one-size-fits-all approaches—because we are all different. What works for one person may not work for another. That's why a rigid 900- to 1200-calorie-per-day diet paired with vigorous exercise is ineffective for 95% of people.

These programs rely on counting calories or points, eliminating entire food groups until you lose weight, and then going back to "normal" eating—which can create an unhealthy relationship with food and lead to yo-yo dieting.

The majority of weight loss experts agree on some general principles that apply to everyone: drink more water, exercise, be mindful of what and how much you eat, get quality sleep, and reduce stress.

Before starting a diet, many people binge on foods they think they won't be able to eat for a while. The binge-and-overeat cycle—where people diet strictly during the day and overeat at night or restrict themselves all week and then indulge on the weekend—becomes their new norm. Dieting fuels disordered eating.

And here's the paradox: when we fail on a diet, we blame ourselves, not the diet. We start to distrust ourselves around food. We feel ashamed and guilty and say terrible things to ourselves, like, *You don't deserve to eat.*

There are hundreds of organized weight loss programs out there. Many claim rapid weight loss and lasting results. These programs often rely on excessive calorie restriction, the elimination of carbohydrates or fat, and over-exercising. And because people put in tremendous effort, they appear to lose weight quickly.

While participants appreciate the support, structure, and accountability these programs provide, and they may gain some basic nutrition knowledge, the reality is that these programs focus primarily on counting calories or points. This can create an unhealthy relationship with food and even pose health risks, as their main emphasis is rapid weight loss. Endocrinologists warn that rapid weight loss can be detrimental to our health because it can lead to nutritional deficiencies, which cause inflammation, as well as electrolyte imbalances (see Figure 1). These programs also fail to prioritize the healthiest food choices and do not consider factors such as body composition, digestion, sleep, mood, and energy levels.

"...although short-term weight loss after obesity is associated with immediate metabolic health improvements, the gut microbiota requires longer-term maintenance of weight loss to return to a non-obese state."

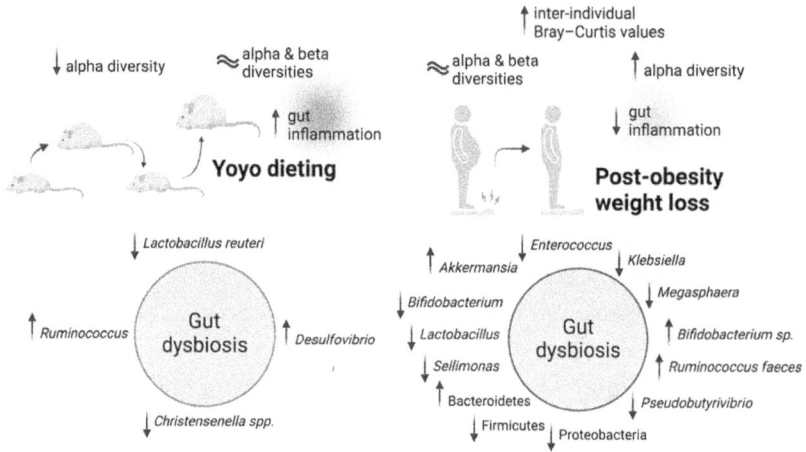

(Figure 1) Yoyo Dieting, Post-Obesity Weight Loss, and Their Relationship with Gut Health By Kate Phuong-Nguyen, Sean L. McGee, Kathryn Aston-Mourney, Bryony A. Mcneil, Malik Q. Mahmood, and Leni R. Rivera. MDPI article published 19 September 2024.

Dieting often leads to self-sabotage and overeating. The cycle of dieting and overeating ultimately slows down metabolism, making weight loss increasingly difficult.

This conclusion comes from research comparing body composition in such scenarios. Clients at a weight-loss clinic were first measured when they initially lost weight. They followed a strict regimen—akin to *The Biggest Loser*—consisting of an extreme diet and boot camp-style exercise. While effective in the short term, it was incredibly difficult to maintain.

Here's what happens when people restrict calories:

When they lose 40 pounds, their weight loss consists of 20 pounds of fat, 12 pounds of water, and 8 pounds of muscle. This means that, alongside fat loss, they also lose muscle mass, which requires dedicated exercise to rebuild.

These same clients "fell off the wagon" after strict dieting and excessive exercise. When they returned to the clinic after regaining the weight, the composition of the weight regained consisted of 24 pounds of fat, 16 pounds of water, and 0 pounds of muscle.

Why is this? This is mainly because when people take a break from their "impossibly healthy lifestyle," they typically don't go to the gym.

As a result, muscle mass decreases, and metabolism slows down further. This makes each subsequent weight loss attempt harder than the last. According to studies, muscle mass burns more calories than fat tissue not only during exercise but also during rest. When people follow a diet that is dialed in on reducing calories, including calories from protein, their body breaks down their own muscle tissue for fuel, decreasing overall muscle during a diet. Fewer muscle mass bodies burn fewer calories.

Here are the calculations. From 40 pounds of overall weight, Tamara lost 8 pounds of muscle during her first diet that was not focused on building muscle. Eight pounds of muscle loss slowed down her metabolism by approximately 4.5 to 7.0 kcal/lb per day. This means that her body needed from 36 to 56 calories per day less after her first diet. (Elia, 1992)

Then Tamara gained 40 pounds of weight back, without regaining her initial muscle mass. When people stop engaging muscles, their mass decreases over even a relatively short period of time. During her second diet, Tamara loses 40 pounds of overall weight and 8 more pounds of muscle mass. Now, her body needs from 72 to 112 fewer calories per day. If Tamara repeats the yo-yo process a third time, it will leave her body needing from 106 to 168 calories less. So if Tamara used a 1200-calorie diet to lose her first 40 pounds, after her third diet, she needs 1128 to 1088 calories per day to achieve the same result.

When we start working together my clients sometimes can't remember how many dieting attempts they made. And very often, they report that they gain weight while eating very little as a result of yo-yo dieting. (If you enjoy reading scientific papers, please check the References section to explore the research supporting the conclusions in this book.)

There is life beyond dieting. We already know the solution: we can live in a healthy body through a holistic approach. This is what this book is about—a sustainable, low-effort, healthy lifestyle that you can maintain consistently, prioritizing steady progress over perfection.

A holistic approach addresses the unique combination of contributing and balancing factors in your lifestyle while incorporating a mind-body connection.

If you need to lose weight, it should not be about dieting. It should be about eating for health and longevity—choosing foods that make you feel satisfied, happy, and energized.

I'm *not* going to lay out a step-by-step weight loss program in this book because such a program should be personalized to your unique body chemistry.

And even if I gave you the perfect strategy, you might struggle to follow through without one key factor—your mindset. Your mindset is the foundation of your ability to stay on track and maintain results.

A winning mindset begins with open-mindedness and teachability. Your attitude and willingness to do things differently, combined with a personalized strategy, will help you lose weight, maintain results, and feel young, energetic, and enthusiastic.

Body weight is one of the most debated topics out there. Is being skinny always healthy? Is being overweight always unhealthy? I'm not here to argue about personal preferences when it comes to body shape. My goal is to help you achieve the ideal weight where *your body feels* its best. For every person, the ideal weight is different, depending on factors such as height, muscle mass, bone structure, gender, and metabolism.

Personally, my *ideal weight* is when I feel light, healthy, energized, and excited to see myself in the mirror.

Imagine going on vacation without worrying about how you look. No more irritability. Better relationships with the people around you. Imagine the freedom of choosing outfits based on what you want to wear—grabbing a swimsuit without hesitation.

You'll have more energy. You'll have more time—because you'll become more productive and efficient. You'll manage stress better and continue losing weight in a sustainable way.

You can change right now. All you need is honesty, open-mindedness, and willingness.

A UNIVERSAL LAW: SOMETHING FOR SOMETHING

If you want to gain something, you need to give something. If you want to change, you need to have skin in the game. Successful people invest in coaching to reach the next level—starting with a significant financial commitment. By putting their skin in the game, they ensure they follow the instructions and do the work.

Twelve-step programs are free, yet they only work for those who have already paid—through suffering, humiliation, and defeat. Defeat makes them ready to listen, accept guidance, and follow the steps.

Honesty is one of the pillars of success. Ask yourself: Are you willing to be honest, open-minded, and committed to doing the work outlined in this book?

The truth will set you free. Honesty will bring awareness to what's holding you back.

An open mind allows you to see new perspectives. A shift in perspective is a miracle—one that enables change. Open your mind to allow new ideas to shape a low-effort, healthy lifestyle that you can sustain—so you can enjoy your strong body, high physical and mental energy, and long-lasting well-being.

Willingness means committing, persevering, and staying dedicated to doing what it takes to become the best version of yourself.

And just know this: you can turn your situation around faster than you think. You will astonish yourself. I did. From the inside, the process may feel slow, but you'll see the wonder in the eyes of people who haven't seen you for a couple of months.

If you're feeling like a failure—trapped in the cycle of yo-yo dieting —or even if your behavior feels borderline addictive, know that you can turn your life around quickly.

All it takes is honesty, open-mindedness, and the willingness to take small, consistent steps every day until you reach your goal.

Allow yourself to want more. You will surprise yourself with how persistent you can be. You'll push through the discomfort of those first steps. Your dream won't let you give up.

All I wish for you right now is to allow yourself to become the greatness that you already are.

I invite you to work with this book. First, just read it. Then, read it a second time and implement all the suggestions.

Pillar 1:

Setting a Goal and Creating a New Self-Image

CHAPTER 1
YOU ARE WHAT YOU THINK
OF YOURSELF

*"People with goals succeed because they
know where they're going."*
– Earl Nightingale

WHO DO YOU HAVE TO BE TO ACHIEVE YOUR GOAL?

When you learn this strategy for goal achievement, you will become unstoppable. Think about traveling—you need a clear destination and an exact date of arrival. If you state your destination vaguely, saying something like, "I'm supposed to be in America in the fall," nobody can issue you a ticket. But if you say, "Boston, MA, USA, on October 15th," you will get exactly what you need.

You wouldn't argue about the importance of being precise when booking a trip, right? The same principle applies to achieving anything in life. When you know exactly what you want, the Universe will align the right circumstances, introduce you to the right people, and open doors at the right time to help you get there.

When I start working with a new client, I ask about their goals in regards to their well-being. They usually say something similar to *I want to feel good,* or *I want to feel sexy again.* These are wishes, as goals they are as vague as *I'm supposed to be in America in the fall.* To feel sexy is a great desire, and you need to attach a feeling to your goal as well, but to transform a desire into a goal, it needs the exact parameters, specificity, and a deadline.

By December 31 of this year, I want to fit into the clothes that I wore 3 years ago. I want to play squash again without needing to catch my breath after each pass in two months from now. Those goals can be measured and identified when you reach them. Precisely knowing what you want, you can create a plan on how to get it and divide it into attainable pieces. Then, you can measure your progress every now and then and correct your actions if necessary.

There are a couple of things to consider when you decide what you want regarding your body. First, your body needs to be loved, accepted, and respected on its own terms. Look at your body from a place of love and imagine the best version of yourself.

Keep in mind that *losing one pound per week is an ideal scenario.* Often, your body needs time to adjust before it can lose more weight. In other words, be patient with your weight loss journey—just as you would be if you were teaching your great-great-grandmother to use social media!

The second thing to consider is that your goal has to speak to both the logical and emotional parts of your brain. Let's start with emotions. Ask yourself:

- *How do you imagine you will feel when you reach your goal?*
- *What do you want to do once you achieve it?*
- *What new experiences will be possible for you?*

Don't be afraid to dream big. Dreaming is not a waste of time—it's essential. Your goal should be something you *really, really* want. Don't hold back from desiring something that ignites a fire inside you, something that makes you willing to do whatever it takes to achieve it.

WHAT DO YOU WANT TO BE ABLE TO DO WHEN YOU REACH YOUR GOAL?

Sometimes people—not saying it's you—hesitate to dream because they were conditioned to believe that dreaming is selfish. They confuse their personal desires with the expectations of others.

When my husband and I became caretakers for his mother after she suffered a stroke, I witnessed firsthand how people-pleasing can interfere with personal recovery. A kind occupational therapist asked my mother-in-law what activities she would like to return to once she regained her strength. My mother-in-law, Tatiana, was a deeply responsible woman. She looked at me and said, "I want to be able to help my children around the house."

Tatiana was a brilliant businesswoman raised by her grandmother —a woman who dedicated her life to caring for her daughter, granddaughter, and great-grandson. Looking back, I doubt that Tatiana truly wanted to spend her regained strength doing household chores. However, having been raised by a selfless caretaker, she felt compelled to follow in her footsteps. Wanting to feel useful and connected to her family, she asked the therapist to help her regain her muscle tone so she could wash dishes, dust, vacuum, and do laundry.

With a goal that wasn't truly hers, my mother-in-law tried to exercise but saw little progress. Because she wasn't genuinely excited about it, Tatiana didn't put much effort into regaining her strength and range of motion. If she had found the courage to acknowledge her real desires and state them clearly, she would have approached occupational therapy with a sense of purpose—and that purpose would have changed her results.

Please, be brave. Allow yourself to express your true desires and dream big.

If mental chatter and self-judgment arise the moment you start thinking about what you want, try this: put on some relaxing music, make a cup of your favorite tea or coffee, light a candle, and start writing your wish list. Give yourself 20 to 60 minutes without distractions, and simply allow your deepest desires to surface. You have this one life. What do you want to achieve before it's over? If anything were possible, what would you choose?

And now you can come back to your goal.

YOUR GOAL

Please set your health goal here:

Date: _____

I feel:

_____

_____

I do:

_____

_____

Example: December 31, I feel safe, serene, at peace, and light as I run 3 km in less than 20 minutes. I feel the fresh, crisp air, my lungs expanding and contracting as I run. I weigh 125 pounds, and it is amazing to feel my body moving without pain. I love it.

Now, we need to update our internal self-image—the way we unconsciously see ourselves, our personality, and what we are capable of achieving.

If you are surprised when people compliment you, your internal self-image needs an update. If you feel that you lack confidence, your internal self-image needs an update. If you find yourself saying negative things like, "I have no willpower. I'm lazy. I let myself go. I'm a terrible eater," then your self-image *definitely* needs an update.

Now, let's create the best version of you—the version that has already achieved your goal.

To change your body, you must go through a gradual yet complete psychic transformation.

If you want to stop struggling with your weight and body image, you have to create a new version of yourself—one in which you are at your ideal healthy weight and in love with your body. If you try to change your diet and start a new exercise program without updating your self-image, you will keep falling back into old patterns.

Any external change without internal mindset work is a waste of time and effort.

In this book, I will lay out all the strategies to help you change habits at the root cause level—saving you years of frustration and helping you build a strong foundation for your new healthy lifestyle.

Let's dive into the cause of all good and evil.

We can see what's going on inside your mind by your current results. Your body, health, relationships, prosperity, and success all reveal how your mindset operates. As Bob Proctor puts it, "Success is 5% strategy and 95% mindset."

Your mindset can be your greatest ally or your worst enemy.

HOMEOSTASIS: THE INVISIBLE FORCE THAT KEEPS YOU STUCK

First, I want to share a fascinating fact that completely changed how I viewed mindset work.

I once witnessed a French-Canadian family of four win a couple of million dollars in the lottery. This was a *huge* amount of money in the 1990s—enough for each of them to buy at least two beautiful homes in Canada. They happily moved out of their apartment building. Two years later, they were back in the same apartment, living under the same circumstances as before.

Did you know that the vast majority of lottery winners return to their previous financial situation within two years of winning?

This is how the set point works. Its goal is to always bring things back as they were. A drastic change, even when it's absolutely positive, feels uncomfortable. Lottery winners often report that when they move to a new house, they feel rejected by the community they were in before, as well as by the new community. They feel out of place. Subconsciously, they make decisions that bring them back to the old patterns that make them feel comfortable.

Set point works just like the heating-cooling system in a building. If it's too hot outside, the system will cool down the temperature inside. If it's too hot outside, the system will heat up to bring the temperature to the same set point.

The same mechanism operates when people regain weight after successfully losing 20 pounds. It keeps people stuck in a cycle of yo-yo dieting—losing weight only to gain it back again—because their body and mind are accustomed to carrying extra pounds.

This mechanism is also responsible for 92% of failed New Year's resolutions, repeatedly falling in love with the wrong kind of person, and even self-sabotaging relationships.

This powerful force is called **homeostasis** or **set point**. Walter Bradford Cannon studied homeostasis extensively. In his 1932 work *The Wisdom of the Body*, he described it as the body's natural tendency to maintain stability.

According to the *Encyclopedia Britannica*, homeostasis is *"A self-regulating process by which biological systems tend to maintain stability."*

However, homeostasis isn't just physiological—it's also psychological. Our nervous system is incredibly complex, and homeostasis isn't always achieved in a positive or healthy way. It depends on a person's internal *programming*. For example, I once worked with a stunningly beautiful actor who constantly referred to herself as "a terrible eater" because she enjoyed cheese, bagels, and ethnic cuisine. Every time she lost weight for a role, she gained it right back as soon as filming wrapped because, as she put it, "...you know, I'm a terrible eater."

Her self-perception—believing she was a "terrible eater"—became her homeostasis. This belief triggered guilt, shame, and compulsive food-seeking behavior as an unconscious way of restoring the familiar status quo. Even though her eating habits weren't objectively "terrible," her deep-seated belief reinforced this identity. Any attempt to challenge it would disrupt her homeostasis, making her uncomfortable —because these beliefs formed the foundation of her self-image. For her to maintain homeostasis, she had to uphold the identity of a terrible eater—whether she consciously wanted to or not.

That is how people find themselves scrolling through social media instead of implementing their award-winning business plan, gambling away their family savings, using alcohol or drugs to sabotage a big promotion, or bingeing on food that leaves their body in pain the next day—only to ask themselves, *Why did I do that?*

SELF-SABOTAGE

Many people get stuck in the cycle of losing weight only to gain it back. This happens because, as they get closer to their goal, their homeostasis pulls them back to the familiar "safety" of excess weight and the struggle that comes with it.

- The struggle with weight becomes part of their identity— and if they lose that extra weight, they also lose a part of themselves. Losing a part of oneself is scary. Change is scary. The future is scary. They don't know exactly what they'll gain, but they know exactly what they'll lose. They might lose the luxury of feeling invisible and wearing comfortable, baggy clothes. They might suddenly attract more attention.
- They might have to spend money on a new wardrobe. They might need to step out of their comfort zone and talk to strangers.

This psychological mechanism is known as hidden benefits—the unconscious rewards that come from staying the same. Homeostasis has many hidden benefits.

That's why you need to create a clear and detailed image of your future self—one that reassures your homeostasis that there is nothing to fear when you achieve your goal.

And you must be willing to say goodbye to the old version of yourself.

If you try to change your diet and start a new exercise program without updating your self-image, you will keep falling back into old patterns. To change your results permanently, you have to go through a gradual psychic transformation—otherwise, the yo-yo cycle will never end.

When we set a big, exciting goal, it disrupts homeostasis. Our nervous system unconsciously activates mechanisms like procrastination, perfectionism, and self-sabotage to restore balance and return us to the familiar.

We must become aware of the limitations associated with our old self (our homeostasis) and make changes gradually—just 10% at a time.

If we attempt a 100% transformation all at once, the nervous system experiences stress, stress triggers pain, and the limbic brain pulls us back into the old "safety zone" by sabotaging our efforts.

Consider this: There are roughly 100 waking hours in a week. If you deliberately focus on changing just 10 hours per week, leaving the rest of your routine unchanged, homeostasis won't be alarmed. This is how you create a low-effort, healthy lifestyle that you can consistently maintain—with steady, sustainable progress.

Homeostasis ("stability through constancy," as Walter Cannon defines it) originates from laboratory-based experimental physiology pioneered by Claude Bernard. It shows that living systems tend to maintain functionality through consistency. For example, your body automatically regulates its temperature to keep you stable, regardless of external conditions.

The same principle applies to your nervous system. Let's say you've moved to a new city and received a big promotion—congratulations! But now, your homeostasis is threatened. What's your usual form of self-sabotage? Overspending? Overeating? Drinking too much? Entering another toxic relationship?

As your awareness expands, you'll begin to recognize that every aspect of your life—your health, happiness, finances, and relationships —has been shaped largely by your own unconscious patterns.

The good news? Homeostasis is not the only force at play.

The only mechanism capable of overriding homeostasis is neuroplasticity—which I'll explain in detail in the next chapter.

But first things first: You need to create a new version of yourself to reach your goal.

CREATING YOUR NEW SELF

Your results flow from the core of your identity—who you believe yourself to be.

The concept of self-image was first developed by Dr. Maxwell Maltz and described in his book *Psycho-Cybernetics*. As a plastic surgeon, he noticed something fascinating: Some of his patients experienced dramatic personality shifts after cosmetic surgery, along with improvements in their confidence and life circumstances. Others, despite looking entirely different, felt the same and continued experiencing the same struggles as before. This revealed a powerful truth: Self-image is not about how we look—it's about how we *see* ourselves.

Your environment shaped your self-image as you were growing up, but the good news is that you can always change it. You can choose a new self-image that aligns with your goals. And when you do, success will come naturally—because you'll no longer be fighting against the old version of yourself.

When I was getting out of my yo-yo dieting cycle, I later realized that I saw myself as weighing 300 pounds, even though my actual weight was around 154 pounds. I was afraid to eat because I believed I had an insatiable appetite. I didn't allow myself to eat the foods my body craved and instead tried to eat very little—until I snapped, overate, and made more promises to myself to start a very strict diet tomorrow. I was stuck in this cycle for 14 years.

It took a great amount of willpower to let go of my fear of food and eat only when I was physically hungry. I kept a food journal to track what I ate, and it turned out that my appetite was normal and that I ate a healthy amount of food. I also discovered that I actually preferred natural, high-quality foods over processed ones.

It was my self-image that kept me stuck in the cycle of overeating and restricting for all those years. When I let go of all the judgments about my eating habits and updated my self-image to reflect someone who ate healthily when hungry and in appropriate portions, I was able to lose 30 pounds—and keep it off.

As my self-image changed, so did my life and environment. I saw myself as a more confident person, and as a result, I started getting promotions at work. I saw myself as someone worthy of love, and I allowed myself to receive it. I was gifted with a family and a child.

Only you can change your self-image. The more closely your self-image aligns with the best version of yourself, the more your circumstances and environment will shift to match that new version. If you want to achieve certain results, you need to adopt the behaviors that create those results. If you want to adopt those behaviors, you need to cultivate the right feelings that trigger them. If you want to feel the right feelings, you need to develop the right thoughts. And if you want to have the right thoughts, you need to become the kind of person to whom those thoughts naturally occur.

Another way of saying this is that if we focus less on what we want to do and have and more on who we want to be, everything starts to flow more easily.

Instead of thinking: *Have* → *Do* → *Be*
we need to reverse it: *Be* → *Do* → *Have*

For example, instead of thinking:

*"Once I lose the weight, then I'll have the confidence,
I'll be more outgoing, and I'll meet my future partner."*

Approach it as:

*"I see myself as a confident person, and I attract
a partner who appreciates me for who I am."*

Be a confident person now.

So, who do you need to be? Who is the person who naturally does the things you want to do? What kind of person would have access to the kind of outcomes you want?

- How do they carry themselves?
- What personality traits do they possess?
- How do they dress?
- How do they show up in a room?

THE HOLLYWOOD BODY METHOD

- How do other people feel when they're around them?
- What thoughts do they think?
- What do they believe?
- What do they ignore?
- What do they value?

Use the Who Do You Need To Be Worksheet to spend time reflecting on these and other important questions about updating your self-image.

To access the
Who Do You Need To Be Worksheet

SCAN THE QR CODE:

SCAN ME

WHO DO YOU NEED TO BE TO ACHIEVE YOUR GOAL?

When we focus less on what we want to *do* and *have* and more on who we want to *be*, everything starts to flow more easily.
What type of person naturally does the things you want to do or easily creates the outcomes you desire?
Spend some time with these questions. Don't rush this exercise.

How do you carry yourself? (Example: *With great confidence.*)

_____

_____

How do you dress? (Example: *Neat and stylish.*)

_____

_____

What personality traits do you possess? (Example: *Warmness, account-ability, responsibility, kindness, generosity, optimism.*)

_____

_____

How do you measure your value? (Example: *I am valuable.*)

_____

_____

How do you show up in a room? (Example: *With a smile and an open heart.*)

_____

_____

How do other people feel when you're around them? (Example: *People feel better in my energy.*)

_____

_____

What thoughts do you think? (Example: *I think that I have an amazing life, that anything is possible, and that I am ready to do all it takes to fulfill my dreams.*)

_____

_____

What do you believe? (Example: *I believe in love, and kindness, and every day I get exactly what I need for my growth.*)

_____

_____

What do you ignore? (Example: *I ignore negativity, gossip, complaining.*)

_____

_____

What do you value? (Example: *I value friendship, integrity, and being true to myself.*)

_____

_____

What do you do when you face a challenge? (Example: *I think that challenges are necessary stepping stones that strengthen me.*)

_____

_____

What do you know to be true about yourself? (Example: *I am capable. I have done a million difficult things in life that have made me stronger. I can overcome challenges.*)

What do you do to take care of yourself? (Example: *I experience life through this body here on Earth. I take care of my mind through daily prayer, meditation, and choosing the right thoughts. I take care of my body by nourishing it with good, healthy food, exercising, breathing fresh air, and sleeping well.*)

ALTER EGO

You can also use an alter ego. This concept is widely used by actors, performers, and athletes. It helps shape the person you need to become so that you can start doing the things you want to *do* and ultimately *achieve the results* you *desire*.

You create a character who embodies all the characteristics and abilities you know you need to have to reach your goal.

It can be easier to imagine yourself stepping into a character than seeing yourself with different characteristics.

A famous example of an alter ego is the late Kobe Bryant's Black Mamba—a fierce, agile, and combative persona. Beyoncé created Sasha Fierce, a stage persona embodying sensuality, confidence, and aggression.

You can create your own alter ego by drawing inspiration from an existing person or a fictional character that resonates with you. Whenever you need strength or confidence, channel your Wonder Woman alter ego to rise to the occasion.

Use the Alter Ego Worksheet to gain clarity and develop an alter ego that aligns with your goal.

To access the
Alter Ego Worksheet

SCAN THE QR CODE:

SCAN ME

LUCKY CHARM

After creating your alter ego, make it more tangible with a lucky charm. This will help you tap into your alter ego whenever you need it.

A lucky charm is a powerful psychological tool because it has deep roots in our subconscious. Since the beginning of civilization, tangible objects have been used to symbolize commitment and transformation. Family artifacts were passed down to preserve an ancestral force. From shamanism to modern religions, objects have played a central role in initiation ceremonies—such as the cross in Christianity or bead bracelets in Buddhism.

Similarly, 12-step programs use chips and medallions to confirm commitment and celebrate milestones. Even in academic settings, when people graduate from a university, they are often given objects symbolizing their achievement and their belonging to an institution.

A lucky charm is a talisman that holds deep personal meaning. Carrying it with you serves as a constant reminder of that meaning, reinforcing your commitment whenever you need it. In neuroscience, a lucky charm functions as a trigger for a specific emotional state.

To fully tap into the power of your lucky charm, choose it carefully. It should be something small and portable—such as a piece of jewelry or a small stone—that you can easily carry with you at all times.

Program your lucky charm with your goal by stating your intention and visualizing yourself achieving it. Imagine how it feels to live the healthy life you desire or to embody your alter ego. Hold your lucky charm and connect it to the emotions associated with your success. This process "activates" the charm, linking it to your transformation.

Carry your lucky charm with you. Whenever you need to tap into your alter ego or remind yourself why you are changing your habits, touch it and recall the feeling of your success.

KEY POINTS:

1. State your Big Goal.
2. Decide who you need to be to reach your highly desirable big goal.
3. Craft a suitable self-image.
4. Identify how homeostasis may be working against you and how you can make it work for you.
5. Describe yourself in your new goal, with every detail, to calm down your homeostasis and avoid setbacks.
6. Create an Alter Ego.
7. Use a Lucky Charm for reinforcement of your new self-image.

CHAPTER 2

YOUR BEST FRIEND AND YOUR WORST ENEMY—THE CONSCIOUS MIND AND THE AUTOMATIC MIND

"I am, indeed, a king because I know how to rule myself."
– Pietro Aretino

YOUR BEST FRIEND AND YOUR WORST ENEMY

You have your delicious goal—one that fires you up with the determination of a five-year-old on a mission to fill their Halloween bag with candy.

Some days, you step into the new version of yourself and feel unstoppable. On other days, your old self takes charge, and you feel like the worst person in the world.

"What the f… is wrong with me?" you ask.

Many things!

This chapter will help you understand why you do what you do—and why you don't do what you say you'll do… You know what I mean.

I can't even count how many times I started a new healthy eating and exercise regimen, only to have it last for a few days…or a few hours…or sometimes just minutes. I would wake up determined, but before I knew it, I was skipping my morning run and eating ice cream for breakfast, lunch, and dinner. Seriously, I did. That was one of my successful experiments! Which, of course, left me feeling guilty and ashamed. I couldn't even catch myself in the act of doing things I didn't want to do. It felt like a tornado: one moment, clear skies, and the next—*bam!*—devastation, ruins and regrets.

I labeled this behavior as "bad," "weak," or "lazy."

And if you find yourself doing things you don't want to do—while calling yourself names—let me tell you:

You are none of those things. You are not a bad, immoral, or weak person just because you struggle to exercise or resist sugar.

Once you understand why we don't do the "good" things we want to do and instead do the "bad" things we don't want to do, you'll be able to control your behavior.

MEET YOUR BEST FRIEND AND YOUR WORST ENEMY: THE CONSCIOUS AND THE AUTOMATIC MIND

Mind can only be regarded, for scientific purposes, as the activity of the brain. Our mind is structured in a way that makes permanent change hard—unless, of course, you've been conditioned to believe that change is good and easy.

But here's the good news: You can absolutely trick your mind into changing your habits, avoiding self-sabotage, and making lasting changes faster.

We repeat old unhealthy habits because of what's going on inside our brain. We think we are in control of our minds, but the reality is the opposite—our mind controls us. Take a moment to understand how to rewire your brain to stop behaviors that no longer serve you.

Our prefrontal cortex controls **conscious thinking and new behaviors**. It is responsible for:

- Reasoning
- Maintaining social appropriateness
- Decision-making
- Personality expression
- Other complex cognitive behaviors.

Conscious thinking processes new information, assesses its relevance and meaning for us at the moment, and takes action if required.

Let's consider the example of Yasmina to illustrate this point.

Yasmina's conscious mind was fully engaged when she faced the reality of carrying around an extra 95 pounds. She felt low on energy, lacked confidence, and decided to eliminate carbs from her diet.

I am not eating carbs. I am not eating sweets. I am losing weight, she promised herself.

For a few days, she was present and aware of her decision. It felt doable. She stayed away from carbs.

But then came Wednesday. A stressful situation at work triggered her automatic thinking, and suddenly, she found herself in the kitchen, rationalizing, *Maybe I can have two squares of dark chocolate with maltitol. That wouldn't technically violate my diet... Okay, just two squares of dark chocolate.*

Ten minutes later...

After finishing the entire chocolate bar, she thought: *I ruined my diet. I might as well eat everything I've been craving for the past few days, and just restart my diet tomorrow.*

The automatic mind repeats all the actions we've *already assessed* and reinforced in the past. Once we've made a decision about something a few times, our brain automates that process, so the conscious mind doesn't have to check in again.

The **automatic** mind is at work when we brush our teeth, tie our shoes, walk to work, growl in traffic, or react negatively to a comment. This type of **thinking,** which **is part of our limbic system,** is where habits and unconscious behaviors—including repetitive thoughts—are stored.

The automatic mind takes over when we:

- Always prepare for the worst
- Eat when stressed
- Check our phones anytime we have a spare second
- Scroll through social media instead of completing an assignment
- Turn on the TV in the evening

The automatic *mind is a habit-making machine* because habits conserve brain energy. This is why you may find yourself stopping at the same fast food restaurant and ordering huge portions—even when you're not physically hungry. Your automatic brain tells you, "We always stop here and order this."

Our brain associates certain places and situations with specific behaviors, such as:

- Reaching for something sweet after a meal.
- Eating popcorn at the movies.
- Having a donut with coffee on the way to work.

When the prefrontal cortex is engaged, it consumes a lot of energy. To conserve energy, the body prefers switching to habitual actions and reactions. This is why people who want to lose weight often reach for a piece of cake before they can stop themselves.

Our conscious thinking burns a significant amount of energy. Think about how tired and hungry you feel after learning a new skill or taking an exam—that's because engaging conscious thinking requires a great deal of effort.

In contrast, automatic thinking *is highly energy-efficient.* The brain conserves energy as much as possible—just in case we need to run from a predator or walk miles to gather food. That's why it constantly creates habits around thoughts or actions that we repeat.

The downside of automatic thinking is that once an action or thought becomes a habit, it's difficult to be aware of it.

Becoming mindful is key! When we're on autopilot, we end up making old, unhealthy, self-sabotaging choices.

There's a useful acronym in the 12-step program that describes moments of vulnerability—when people are most likely to experience setbacks:

HALT = Hungry, Angry, Lonely, Tired

When we experience HALT, our brain switches to the limbic system to save energy. The limbic system, in turn, activates automatic behaviors, bringing back all the old bad habits that come with it.

Please refer to the Mindfulness vs. HALT strategy to help you break out of autopilot, become more intentional with your thoughts and behaviors, and cultivate new, healthier habits and patterns.

To access the
Mindfulness vs. HALT strategy

SCAN THE QR CODE:

SCAN ME

NEUROPLASTICITY

In his 1949 book *The Organization of Behavior: A Neuropsychological Theory*, Canadian neuropsychologist Donald Hebb stated: "Neurons that fire together, wire together." Our brain cells connect with one another through the release of neurotransmitters, which are chemicals that allow communication between neurons. When one neuron fires and another receives the signal, it forms a neural pathway.

With frequent connections, neural pathways strengthen. Over time, communication between those same cells becomes faster, and with enough repetition, the behavior becomes automatic. This is the foundation of habits and the automatic mind.

It's why we learn through repetition and practice—starting with holding, crawling, walking, and repeating the same movements over and over again. Eventually, these actions become automatic. Unless there's an injury, people don't have to remember how to walk every morning—they just get up and walk.

"Muscle memory" is another term for the principle that "Neurons that fire together, wire together." It refers to neural pathways in the brain that strengthen with repetition. When a movement is practiced enough times, we perform it automatically—no conscious thinking required.

All of your habits are stored within the structure of your brain.

Since the brain creates neural pathways for everything we repeatedly do, breaking a habit—like eating sugary snacks at 3 PM or snacking on chips while watching TV—requires rewiring those pathways. To successfully replace unhealthy habits, you must stop reinforcing behaviors that no longer serve you and start repeating actions that move you closer to your goal.

With enough repetitions, your brain will eventually make those actions automatic—that is how we create new, healthier habits. You've probably heard that it takes about 21 days to form a new habit. However, an Australian study suggests that people actually need three times as much time to establish a habit.

You are reading this book because you want to know the truth. I don't want you to expect that if you go to the gym for three weeks in a row, you'll continue going automatically. That expectation is a setback in the making. People in 12-step programs are told to keep coming back for 90 days. After 90 days, newcomers receive a red chip—a reminder to stay vigilant about a possible relapse.

What does this mean? It means you need to stop beating yourself up if you miss one workout. You need patience and understanding with yourself in the beginning so you can continue your healthy lifestyle and make healthy habits automatic—repeating them until your last breath. Your health is not a sprint, not even a marathon. It's a long journey, and only death is the finish line. That's why I believe in creating a low-effort, healthy lifestyle that you can maintain consistently.

LIMBIC SYSTEM

I think you should properly meet your limbic system—the mother of automated thinking, one of the oldest systems of our brain, responsible for **emotional and behavioral** responses. In popular literature, it is often referred to as the "lizard brain" or the "caveman brain."

As you can see, I emphasized "**emotional and behavioral** responses"—because first, we think… then we feel… and then we act.

This part of your brain is responsible for your most basic survival functions. The limbic system controls:

- Breathing
- Heart rate
- Body temperature
- Unconscious behaviors (e.g., fight-or-flight responses, feeding, reproduction, and caregiving)

The hippocampus, the brain's memory center, is responsible for neurogenesis and learning new behaviors. The amygdala, on the other hand, plays a central role in our emotions.

Other key components of the limbic system include:

- The hypothalamus: regulating mood, thirst, hunger, and hormone production
- The basal ganglia: controlling movement, learning, reward processing, and habit formation
- The thalamus: relaying sensory information

The structures of the limbic system sit deep in the center of the brain, between the cerebral cortex and the brainstem.

Our limbic system is hardwired with three primary functions: avoid pain, seek pleasure, and expend as little energy as possible.

Just as it was for our prehistoric ancestors, our brain's priority is to keep us alive long enough to mate and pass on our genetic material.

All living things on Earth share this instinct. When horses graze, they eat the grass closest to them. A sunflower grows toward the sun in a straight line. A dog steals the closest piece of food on a buffet table.

Deep within our limbic system, we are programmed to avoid pain, seek pleasure, and conserve energy. So that "delicious goal" you set with the conscious, rational part of your brain is a threat to your limbic system. And anytime you try to deviate from its programming, it fights you.

Four million years ago, pain meant:

- Famine
- Poisonous food
- Freezing temperatures
- Predator
- Competitors who could steal our food

Today, pain is different, but our brain delivers the same message: DANGER!

You might be surprised to learn that boredom, sadness, stress, overwhelm, worry, exhaustion, guilt, and shame trigger the same survival response in the limbic system as famine or freezing temperatures.

When we experience these emotions, the limbic system identifies them as pain and immediately seeks the quickest pleasure to make that pain go away. This is where modern-day "guilty" pleasures come in: alcohol, cigarettes, drugs, gambling, shopping, toxic relationships, social media, and eating highly processed foods like chocolate, chips, cookies, ice cream, and pretzels.

- This part of our brain can sabotage every effort to change for the better because, to the limbic system, old and familiar = safe. *We ate chips before, and we didn't die. Chips = good.*
- *We've never tried this new salad before. We need to stay safe. We eat chips instead of salad.*

The limbic system's duty is to keep you in the familiar, despite your conscious decision to start doing things differently for your own good. That is why we often end up repeating old habits and patterns, even when they hurt us—because, at a deeper level, they are familiar, and to our limbic system, familiarity equals safety and survival.

Our limbic system thrives on familiarity. Anything that didn't kill us in the past is automatically classified as safe. Even new healthy behaviors, no matter how beneficial, are perceived as unsafe simply because they are new. That is where self-sabotage comes from.

On top of that, given that the limbic system controls survival while the prefrontal cortex controls rational decisions (like buying a new car), which do you think carries more weight? Which one do you think wins when they go head-to-head in a fight? That's right; the caveman brain wins—every single time.

If you think about it, this makes perfect sense. Obviously, we want our brain to prioritize survival functions like keeping our heart beating and maintaining body temperature.

However, this hierarchy isn't so helpful when you consider that the limbic system also contains the basal ganglia, where habits reside, while the prefrontal cortex is where we make rational decisions. If you have a habit of heading to the kitchen at night, that habit lives inside the limbic system. When you decide you want to lose weight and sleep better, you engage your very rational prefrontal cortex to break that old habit. Now you've set the limbic system against the prefrontal cortex, and this isn't going to end well for you when you are in a HALT state. Remember how the limbic system always gets priority?

Imagine a Komodo dragon (limbic system) going against a modern man (prefrontal cortex) in a barehanded battle.

And that's exactly what happens when we attempt to break old ingrained habits around food—our limbic system and prefrontal cortex go head-to-head, and the caveman brain almost always wins.

The reality is that despite all our modern scientific advancements, what's driving most of our reactions, thoughts, and choices is still caveman programming.

Given that our caveman brain is in charge most of the time, use the Understanding When Our Limbic System Is Engaged Worksheet to help you switch from automatic thinking to conscious thinking.

To access the
Understanding When Our Limbic
System Is Engaged Worksheet

SCAN THE QR CODE:

SCAN ME

The good news is neuroplasticity—your brain can be rewired through repeated actions. Rejoice! Every time you engage in an action that moves you closer to your goal, you increase the likelihood that you'll do it again. And the opposite is also true—the more you engage in a bad habit, the stronger that habit becomes.

The prefrontal cortex can override the limbic system, but it requires the right strategy. We do this all the time:

- Instead of flipping someone off in traffic, we force a smile and let them pass. We deliver a presentation despite our fear of public speaking. We calmly remind our children to clean their room, instead of losing our temper.

Whether we respond instead of react depends on how strong our willpower is at that particular moment.

WILLPOWER

I want to explain how you can effectively use your willpower to instill new habits. First, understand that willpower is part of conscious thinking, and it resides in the prefrontal cortex. Willpower helps us switch from automatic thinking to intentional thinking and action.

For example, someone who has a habit of opening a bag of potato chips, sitting on the couch, and turning on the TV—because that's their usual way of ending the day—can override that automatic behavior by choosing a banana instead and changing into workout clothes.

That's willpower in action.

Understanding how willpower works is the key to making lasting changes in your behavior.

It's common to feel conflicted about your willpower: sometimes it feels superhuman, and other times it's so weak you want to crawl under a rock. This is not just your perception—you are absolutely right. When you wake up in the morning, your willpower is at 100%— a full bar. But as your day progresses, every social interaction and decision you make drains that energy. Everything from "Should I get married?" or "Should I invest my millions?" to "What color shirt should I wear today?" depletes the prefrontal cortex and, consequently, your willpower.

Then, there comes a moment when your willpower's battery is low.

This usually happens when you are hungry, angry, lonely, or tired. If you are in a HALT state at 3 p.m., you might automatically eat foods you are trying to avoid if they are within reach. When willpower is low, automatic thinking overrides your "healthy" decisions, favoring what's familiar and easy. The truth is, we can't rely on willpower all the time. Willpower is like a rechargeable battery.

This is one of the reasons why, at the end of a long day, a stressed and exhausted Yasmina ends up reaching for sweet and salty snacks with a glass of wine. She knows that cooking a vegetable soup, having a bowl of it, and heading to bed early with a cup of herbal tea and some journaling would be a healthier choice. She knows it would make her feel better and help her lose weight while increasing her energy.

But for her limbic system, indulging in salty peanuts, pretzels, cookies, and shutting down the reasoning part of her brain with wine is the fastest way to escape exhaustion and stress.

To make matters worse, Yasmina starts beating herself up for having weak willpower: *Why am I always so weak? Why can't I say no? Why can't I stay on track? Why can't I do what other people do?*

This self-judgment makes her feel even worse. Now, the limbic system registers that judgment as additional pain and immediately sends her searching for more pleasure to escape it. This means another glass of wine, a bowl of ice cream, and a handful of chocolate-covered pretzels.

So, what should we do instead? How can we win over our limbic system?

With what we've learned about willpower, if you start planning your dinner when your willpower battery is low, chances are you'll end up eating whatever snacks you can find in your kitchen and ordering a pizza. Ordering a pizza is fast and familiar. Your limbic brain has already registered that you didn't die the last time you ate pizza, and the taste was pleasant, so it's safe. Plus, it's an easy and almost immediate choice. Your limbic system demands to be fed now —your low blood sugar is signaling that you are running out of time. *Me eat pizza. Me diet tomorrow. Eat now. We die from hunger. Me feel danger!* screams your limbic system, shutting down your willpower.

This is why willpower is not a long-term solution. Planning and preparation are. Since your willpower is likely to weaken as the day progresses, make sure to plan and prep your balanced breakfast, lunch, and dinner in advance—while your willpower is still strong. I usually plan and prep my food for the week on Saturday morning after breakfast, making sure that dinner takes no more than 10–15 minutes to put together.

Since willpower works like a rechargeable battery, you can restore it by taking time to rest, quenching your thirst, relieving your hunger, connecting to a *Power Greater Than Yourself*, reaching out to a friend or therapist, and becoming mindful.

You can also restart your day at any time. In the next chapters, I explain why allowing yourself to restart your day can "collapse time" and help you reach your goal at lightning speed instead of spending years going in circles.

Willpower works great at the beginning of the day—it's a great starter—but it cannot be used as a long-term strategy. You will learn about the long-term strategy in the following chapters.

HABIT STRUCTURE

The automatic brain creates habits with the same structure: a cue that triggers a repeatable action (routine) followed by a reward. Once a cue triggers an automatic routine, it's hard to stop the behavior before the reward is reached. Your brain is compelled to seek the reward.

Here are some examples of cues that might trigger overeating:

- *Feelings:* A thought that creates worry, stress, or overwhelm; a thought that creates boredom; or a feeling of fatigue at the end of the day.
- *A time of day:* Evening—couch time.
- *Specific people:* "Drinking buddies," "pizza and cannoli with friends," etc.
- *Certain activities:* Going to the movies, watching TV, etc.

The routine is the action triggered by the cue—in this case, overeating highly processed foods.

The reward is either a distraction from stress or boredom or a feeling of connection with friends.

Here's an example of an overeating habit structure:

- Finishing cleaning after dinner and putting the kids to bed at night becomes the cue to open a snack bag and sit in front of the TV. The reward is distraction from feeling tired.

In a bad habit structure, the reward can be something you don't necessarily find pleasant or even beneficial. It may simply be a familiar feeling that soothes your automatic mind. Remember, the limbic system perceives discomfort as pain and familiarity as safety.

As strange as it may seem, when I struggled with binge eating, getting a new, exciting contract and feeling worried about whether I'd be at the top of my game became my cue to overeat until I felt nauseous. I didn't enjoy nausea, but I found it difficult to stop bingeing before reaching that point because nausea was the reward my brain sought—it numbed my excruciating fear of failure. I could only stop eating when I felt sick because that was the signal my brain was looking for.

So how do we escape this cycle when we often don't even notice bad habits repeating until they've run through the full cue-routine-reward structure?

We can break bad habits in several ways:

- **Eliminate some cues:** For example, in 12-step programs, newcomers are advised to avoid certain people, places, and things that trigger their compulsive behavior at the start of their recovery journey.
- **Change the routine:** If the cue is unavoidable—such as evening after work or a stressful situation—you can modify the routine it triggers.
- **Upgrade the reward:** I always prefer upgrading from the false "safety" of nausea to the real comfort of my husband's hugs.

To transform bad habits into good ones, you need to pinpoint their structure. I always recommend tackling one bad habit at a time, starting with the most damaging one. Conquering that first habit will prove that you're capable, allowing you to gradually change all outdated bad habits.

Lilly, for example, realized she was eating too much popcorn and sweets after dinner while watching TV. Watching educational shows with her daughter in the evening was their way of connecting after a long workday, but the snacking was taking a toll on her waistline. This habit had formed over the past couple of years.

The cue was the time of day. This is impossible to change since the night rolls in after the day is over, whether we want it or not.

The routine activity was watching a show and eating snacks.

The reward was feeling connected with her daughter, the idea that *I deserve this after my busy day*, and switching her mind off daily tasks.

Lilly kept the cue and reward and switched the routine: In the evening, after cleaning the kitchen after dinner and prepping the breakfast and lunch for the next day, she served a healthy dessert in the dining room, declaring that the kitchen was "closed" until the following morning. (You can totally borrow this, especially if you have little children who "want a snacky" when it's time to go to bed.) Then her daughter and Lilly prepared for bed, brushed and flossed their teeth, and put on their PJs, making it easy to go to bed right after the show was over while also making it hard to eat more. (I mean, who eats after brushing their teeth?) Lilly also made herself a cup of hot water to drink while cuddling with her daughter in front of the TV.

The reward became even more rewarding: Lilly was absolutely satisfied with her new after-dinner habit. She felt the connection with her daughter and switched her mind off working mode, and on top of that, she was cuddling instead of snacking, completely prepared for her bedtime.

You can use the Habit Structure Worksheet to pinpoint your own cue, routine, and reward of an unhealthy habit you are planning to get rid of.

To access the
Habit Structure Worksheet

SCAN THE QR CODE:

SCAN ME

KEY POINTS:

1. We engage in bad habits without thinking.
2. Our brain activates automatic behavior to save energy.
3. The more you repeat the positive actions, the more automatic they become.
4. Willpower is a rechargeable battery that gets weaker when we are hungry, angry, lonely, and tired.
5. Don't assume that your willpower will be strong at all times, and be prepared for willpower weakness in advance.
6. Pinpoint your bad habit structure to upgrade it.

Pillar 2:

Removing the Old Self-Image

CHAPTER 3
WHO'S IN CHARGE HERE?

"Until you make the unconscious conscious,
it will direct your life, and you will call it fate"
– Carl Jung

WHO'S IN CHARGE HERE?

As you learned in the previous chapter, our brains lie—a lot. We have to stop believing everything they tell us. Habits are powerful because they are automatic. Willpower has gaps you should be prepared for, and while it's great to exercise your willpower to strengthen it, it isn't always reliable. In this chapter, you'll learn more about the evolutionary brain structures that helped us become more efficient at surviving—but that can also become liabilities when you're transforming your body and changing your lifestyle.

DOPAMINE

This neurotransmitter plays a significant role in our brains when we experience cravings. Highly processed foods such as potato chips, candy, and ice cream can feel addictive because they stimulate dopamine receptors. Other activities—such as gambling, shopping, dating, and foraging—also activate the same receptors.

Dopamine is the chemical that drives us to keep acquiring resources, promising that we'll feel good once we've gathered them. However, as soon as we obtain those resources, instead of feeling satisfied, we want more. That's how dopamine works. It's part of the brain's survival reward system, designed to keep us alive by motivating us to gather resources rather than sit still, feeling content with what we already have. Dopamine makes people act.

Dopamine is the evolutionary carrot you never get to eat—a promise of happiness. It doesn't make people happy; rather, it compels them to continue searching for happiness, to keep hunting, working, and accumulating resources. Dopamine's primary function is not to bring happiness but to drive the pursuit of happiness. It exists to get you to move.

When people feel satisfied and content, they stop pursuing. In prehistoric times, stopping could be dangerous, as it could lead to starvation or other survival risks.

The dopamine reward system is activated by things associated with survival:

- Eating sugary and fatty foods provides energy. Feeling excited about a new love interest supports procreation and the survival of the species. Buying new shoes represents resource accumulation.

When people engage in these behaviors, dopamine receptors signal: "Again! Let's do it again! This will make us feel amazing!" But dopamine receptors will never say, "This is it! I feel amazing!" They will never make you feel truly happy, content, or satisfied. Instead, they will always make you want more.

Think back to the last time you gave in to a craving for ice cream, chips, or French fries. Were you satisfied with just one small serving? Or did you want *more*—while feeling guilty at the same time?

The dopamine drive is a chase for pleasure at the cost of well-being. When the brain is on a dopamine-seeking mission, people often act impulsively and feel out of control. They want more—and they are never truly satisfied.

So, how can we manage dopamine-induced cravings? Dopamine production can be balanced with serotonin-, endorphin-, and oxytocin-boosting activities.

What makes you feel good? Usually, these activities don't light up the dopamine receptors, but lead to deep feelings of happiness and satisfaction. These include:

- Spending time outdoors
- Being with loved ones
- Cuddling
- Exercising
- Practicing yoga
- Engaging in creative activities
- Reading
- Being intimate with your partner

You need to plan and prioritize feel-good activities to regulate your dopamine levels, reduce cravings, and prevent compulsive behaviors.

Use the Dopamine vs. Feel-Good Activities Worksheet to guide you.

> To access the
> Dopamine vs. Feel-Good
> Activities Worksheet
>
> SCAN THE QR CODE:
>
> SCAN ME

Become mindful of the gap between how you think you'll feel after eating that piece of chocolate cake and how you actually feel.

To avoid being trapped by dopamine-driven cravings, only eat treats after a balanced meal. If you eat them on an empty stomach, you won't feel satisfied with just one serving—and instead of experiencing joy, you may feel guilt, shame, or anxiety while still wanting more.

It's also vital to recognize false rewards. When you realize that the pleasure dopamine promises doesn't match reality, its spell begins to wear off.

By acknowledging the gap between your expectation (happiness, satisfaction, bliss) and the reality (guilt, shame, anxiety), you force your brain to adjust its expectations—and take back control.

So, when you feel an intense craving for chocolate at 3 p.m., and you feel like you have to get up and get it, promise your brain that you will have a small piece—but only after eating a balanced snack. Remind yourself that dopamine receptors are designed to keep you craving, not to give you satisfaction. Allow yourself the healthiest version of the chocolate, and take control of the process.

MINDSET PROGRAMMING

If you look at how the mind works, the conscious mind is just the tip of the iceberg—the part visible above the water. The largest part of the mind is the subconscious, which controls everything and determines every outcome. The subconscious mind is the emotional mind; it takes everything seriously and does not distinguish between imagined events and reality.

We don't always get what we want, but we always get how we feel about what we want. First, we think. Then, we feel. And then, we act. To change what we do, we need to change what we think. Our thoughts are shaped by our mindset programming, and to reach our goals, we must update that programming.

Our results always reflect our homeostasis paradigm—the mindset we are programmed with. What we actually do, not what we say we will do, reveals our true programming. Now, you have the opportunity to update your old mindset to get better results.

If people try to change their behavior and implement new actions before updating the programming that drives those behaviors, they end up going in circles.

The term **mindset programming** may sound overwhelming—even scary. When I first started working with neuroscience, I pictured a hard drive being rewired inside my skull. But after reprogramming my mind multiple times to achieve different goals, I realized that it's simply about aligning deep subconscious beliefs with new objectives.

It's like putting away your favorite toy train and stuffed T-Rex when you outgrow your "dinosaurs and trains" phase, replacing them with more age-appropriate activities. Recognizing the need for a mindset update is a clear sign that you're evolving to the next level of personal growth. Give yourself a pat on the back!

If you don't update your mindset programming to align with new, healthy habits, maintaining them will be a constant struggle against your willpower. This can lead to willpower fatigue and the activation of the very coping mechanisms you are trying to eliminate.

We are products of our environment. In psychology, this is known as conditioning.

Our subconscious mind is wide open for programming from the moment we are born. Until around ages five to six, it absorbs any information it receives, cementing it as absolute truth. The ideas, limitations, and fears of those around us become deeply embedded because, at that age, we *fully* believe them.

Most of this early programming comes from people who had the best intentions. Typically, beliefs, statements, and habits that helped past generations survive and succeed are passed down to us.

My grandmother, Klara—bless her soul—grew up during wartime. She firmly believed that the more her grandchildren ate, the better. She fed us generous portions, and we wanted to make her happy by finishing everything on our plates. She praised us for taking second and third helpings and proudly cooked the greasiest dishes I had ever tasted.

I still remember the fresh milk drinking competition between me, my brothers, and my cousins at her countryside home. I won the competition—and was rewarded with *severe* diarrhea.

Klara shared her best knowledge, shaped by her survival experience. Eating as much as possible when food was available had helped her survive the war.

But I am fortunate to live in a time of abundance. If I ate *everything* available to me now, I would become obese, my quality of life would decline, and I could develop serious health complications. My job is to recognize old beliefs, thank my grandmother for her wisdom, and let go of outdated conditioning.

Like a hot air balloon, I rise higher and higher as I let go of beliefs, habits, and statements that hold me back.

Outdated Beliefs:

- I'm fat.
- I'm not smart enough.
- I'm too old / too young.
- I'm too busy.
- I don't have strong willpower.
- I'm too slow.
- I'm not a good athlete.
- I'm not a good cook.

Outdated Statements:

- If I put myself first, people will think I'm selfish.
- Things never work out for me.
- I need to do [X, Y, and Z] to be a good daughter / wife / mom / aunt, etc.
- Healthy food is boring.
- Success comes from hard work and sacrifice.
- Beauty is pain.
- Money is evil.

This is how it works. Our brain seeks confirmation of its existing beliefs and statements. This phenomenon, described by Baader-Meinhof—also known as the frequency illusion—occurs when something we've recently learned or noticed seems to appear more frequently. For example, if you start looking for the number 42, you will suddenly notice it everywhere, or if you decide to buy a red car, you might start seeing red cars all over the road.

If you believe that "Success comes from hard work and sacrifice," your thoughts will guide you accordingly. You might pass on an opportunity for what seems like an easy promotion because it feels *too easy.* You may dismiss your years of education and experience, failing to recognize that they *earned* you that promotion. Instead, you will unconsciously seek out opportunities that align with your belief in hard work and sacrifice.

When your new goals and habits conflict with your existing mindset programming, execution becomes difficult. For example, it's hard to enjoy experimenting with new recipes if you believe that you're a bad cook. And making time for the gym five days a week feels nearly impossible if you believe that putting yourself first *is* selfish.

To rise to the level of our desired goals, we need to release what is holding us down—everything that no longer serves us: old beliefs, paradigms, fears, regrets, excuses, feelings of overwhelm, overthinking, doubts, judgments, asking people around you for their opinion, complaining, procrastination, perfectionism. These things once served you. They kept the old version of you safe. But you've outgrown them, just like you outgrew your childhood pajamas.

These patterns drain your energy. They weigh you down. They exhaust you. The problem is that these habits often operate below the level of your conscious awareness.

To free yourself, release the weight. Let go. You'll feel lighter, regain energy, and unlock your full potential.

To change something, you first need to become aware of it. If you remain blind to your own weaknesses, how can you correct them?

Ask yourself:

- *What fears are holding me back?*
- *What limiting statements do I tell myself?*
- *How often do I judge myself or others?*
- *What excuses do I make?*
- *What regrets am I holding on to?*
- *Am I living in the past?*
- *Who or what am I blaming?*

WINNING AGAINST HOMEOSTASIS (SELF-SABOTAGE)

When you ask most people what prevents them from staying on track, they often say: "I don't know!" But the real reason? Homeostasis.

As we discussed previously, homeostasis has one job: to keep things the same.

The struggle with homeostasis is driven by fear. In *Think and Grow Rich* (1937), Napoleon Hill identified six basic fears:

- Fear of Poverty
- Fear of Criticism
- Fear of Ill Health
- Fear of Losing the Love of Someone
- Fear of Old Age
- Fear of Death

The limbic system, which controls emotions and survival instincts, perceives anything unfamiliar as a potential threat. Change feels dangerous—even if it's good for you. Fear convinces you to keep doing what you've always done because staying the same feels safe.

This is why the struggle with homeostasis kicks in when you:

- Plan to lose 20 pounds but never find time for the gym or meal prep.
- Want to learn Spanish but never sign up for a class.
- Dream of writing a novel but can't find the time to start.
- [Insert any goal you've been thinking about for years but haven't taken action on here.]

Releasing these fears is an ancient ritual as vital to your well-being as personal hygiene. Struggle with homeostasis and growth go hand in hand. As soon as our homeostasis is threatened, worry, doubts, indecision, and fears surface. This is the multi-headed dragon you must slay to claim your kingdom.

To become the next version of yourself, you must push through the struggle with homeostasis and face your fears. When you confront them, you grow. You feel lighter. Your energy returns. You become whole again—capable of achieving anything your heart desires.

Don't allow old programming to prevent you from living the life you want to live. The first step is to recognize the doubt, worry, fear, and anxiety, and accept them for what they are. Your doubts, worries, and fears cannot exist alongside your goals without causing conflict. This inner conflict creates ambivalence, which drains your energy—the very energy you need to reach your goal.

Then, let go wholly and completely. Put everything you fear and worry about on a piece of paper, fold it, and release it in a special "Power-Greater-Than-Myself Box." God, Higher Power, or the Universe will take care of your worries and fears. Call the Power Greater Than Yourself whatever feels acceptable to you—it can be your super-ego, Higher Power, Universe, Life's Force, Chi, or Energy. I have used this magical tool, and it helped me step over my fears into my goals and freedom. Don't allow your worries and fears to pull you back into homeostasis. Moving ahead is the answer. With time and practice, the process of recognizing fear, accepting it, releasing it, and moving forward in your decisions becomes faster.

Remember what you were afraid of when you were a child. Darkness? Darkness is scary because it embodies the fear of the unknown. As soon as you switch the light on, darkness shrinks. You can enter the room. There's no monster under the bed. Shine the light on your darkness, get to know your fears, and recognize your doubts and your perceived limits. Who says that you can't be a completely different person? The person you want to be. Every seven to ten years, each cell in your body is replaced by a new one. You are a completely different person every seven to ten years. The only constant in life is change. A set point goes against the laws of the universe. Change is inevitable. You get to choose if your change is progress or regression.

Become familiar with your homeostasis, because it subtly rules our lives unless we become aware of it. You will never hear it saying, "I am afraid of change," or "Change is terrifying because I don't know who I am becoming and what kind of responsibility it brings." No, it has to fool the wise prefrontal cortex, which is not easily deceived. The prefrontal cortex can identify irrational fears and override negative thoughts.

Homeostasis creates sneaky and compelling rationalizations that seem logical. It tells you that what you're thinking of achieving will never work—especially for you—because it's too hard, completely unnecessary, extremely complicated, and definitely not what you need right now.

Homeostasis presents arguments like:

- "We deserve this treat; we'll start again on Monday."
- "We are too busy to make this change; we'll focus on it later when the time is right."
- "It has never worked for us before; it will never work."
- "This is a very special occasion that may never come again, and we won't fully enjoy it unless we indulge."

Have you ever heard something similar in your mind's dialogue? This was homeostasis speaking after you attempted to change.

So, how do you stop the struggle and win over homeostasis?

Here is a four-step process to win the battle between your desire to take steps forward to reach your goals and homeostasis pulling you back into the old and familiar.

1. Become aware of it! Homeostasis always works behind the scenes. As soon as you shine a big, bright light on it and accept it, its power over you begins to weaken.
2. Think about what your future looks like if you let homeostasis rule your life. If you stay in the old and familiar, what does your life look like three years from now? What are you doing? How are you feeling? What have you accomplished?
3. Imagine the best-case scenario. I know—it's not what people usually do. But what if everything works out in the best possible way? Because the Universe is so generous.
4. To keep homeostasis from being alarmed and to avoid self-sabotage and burnout, start changing about 10% of your actions each week. It may seem like 10% isn't enough to create noticeable change, but imagine you have 100 ml of vinegar. Every week, you add 10% water and remove 10% of the total liquid. Little by little, instead of vinegar, you'll have 100 ml of water. The same applies to the habits you want to change. If you adjust just 10% each week, by the end of a year, you will be a completely different person.

In Chapter 5, I will explain in detail how to plan for success to avoid a constant battle with homeostasis.

Homeostasis is always there. However, that doesn't mean it gets to rule your life. With time, as you practice these steps—recognizing homeostasis, acknowledging it, accepting it, imagining what happens if you do nothing, visualizing the best-case scenario, and then changing 10% of your actions at a time—your battles with it will become shorter and shorter, and you will always be the one who wins.

Check out the Letter to Self-Sabotage for help with this.

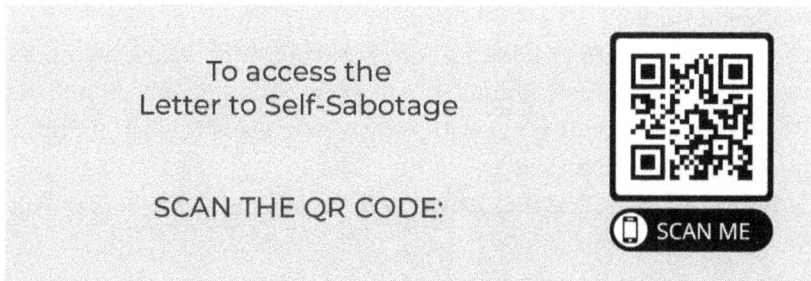

> To access the
> Letter to Self-Sabotage
>
> SCAN THE QR CODE:
>
> SCAN ME

Let go of the **committee of indecision** within you. This quality of character lowers your self-esteem because it keeps you stuck in ambiguity, unable to move forward. High-achieving people make decisions quickly because doing so allows them to receive feedback faster and adjust their course if needed. Indecision, over-planning, and excessive calculations about how to do something just right create anxiety that keeps you stuck. There are no right or wrong decisions—we are not meant to predict the future. Acting on your gut feeling and correcting your course when feedback is received is the best way to move forward.

Until we let go of our mind's judgments and opinions of good and bad, we remain victims of the random, uncontrolled thoughts that bubble into our awareness from the subconscious, constantly swarming around our heads.

Let go of the memories that hold you back. If needed, seek extra help to release trauma and transform it into power. You are not a helpless victim. Trauma happens, but it doesn't have to define you. Maybe the true message of trauma is that you are a strong survivor.

Life is a mystery unfolding in our awareness. Just as there are different interpretations of the past and many ways to change the present, there are countless possible futures. Take your personal opinion out of the situation. Don't engage in guilt, and cancel the punishment—this is how you break free from the yo-yo cycle.

We become free of the world's turbulence as soon as we stop taking our bubbling thoughts so seriously and choose better thoughts that align with the new version of ourselves. This is how we create a healthier, happier self.

Concentrate on your programming and become the person you were meant to be.

The most important thing right now is your mindset. Homeostasis, based on outdated programming, will keep pulling you back into old habits and patterns. It may even present new ways to keep things as they are unless you update it.

Please use the Outdated Beliefs and Statements Worksheet to help you recognize them.

To access the
Outdated Beliefs and Statements
Worksheet

SCAN THE QR CODE:

SCAN ME

HOW TO EASILY ACCOMPLISH WHAT YOU PLANNED

People think that in order to change their results, they need to focus on their actions.

They say, "If I want to lose 20 pounds, I need to eat healthily and go to the gym." Sounds logical, right?

They start acting in a certain way to get specific results:

- "I'll meal prep."
- "I'll put a reminder on my phone to bring my lunch to work!"
- "I'll join the gym."

The new behavior usually works for a few weeks, but then people experience some sort of setback and stop repeating their new habits. They feel disappointed with their behavior but can't seem to stay consistent.

Now that you understand how willpower and the mind work, you may realize that simply wanting something badly enough and relying on willpower alone is not enough to create permanent behavioral change. The root cause of actions lies in the feelings that are fueled by thoughts.

THOUGHT → FEELING → ACTION → RESULT

Feelings are the fuel for actions. When you experience negative emotions—such as boredom, sadness, loneliness, anger, fear, stress, overwhelm, or worry—your behavior often becomes automatic. The limbic system perceives negative emotions as pain and pushes you toward the easiest and most immediate escape, such as scrolling through social media, shopping, or eating. You may even create an emotional "attack" to distract yourself from uncomfortable emotions.

If you engage in this behavior often, it can become a habit that gets triggered automatically. You need to identify the feeling that activates the action.

For example, you may have developed a routine of opening a bag of chips whenever you encounter an issue at work. Before grabbing the chips, you might tell yourself, "I need a snack," but in reality, your limbic system is responding to stress. It perceives feelings of being stuck, worried, or anxious as pain and seeks an immediate way to escape. The action of eating chips becomes a way to avoid the discomfort of those feelings.

You might have repeated this action as a response to those feelings for years, so much so that it became an automatic habit, developing strong neural pathways linking certain emotions at work with the escape of strong tastes in your mouth and dopamine hits from having just one more chip. You might not even notice the connection between the feeling and the action.

Feelings, in turn, have their own source—thoughts. In a way, feelings are an indication of what's going on in your mind. Pleasant thoughts = pleasant feelings; painful thoughts = uncomfortable feelings. This is where the chain starts:

THOUGHT → FEELING → ACTION → RESULT

Feelings are generated by thoughts. The process of developing a feeling as a result of a thought happens so quickly that you may not even notice it. When you feel an uncomfortable emotion—frustration, stress, anger, or worry—and find yourself repeating a pattern you want to break, you need to uncover the thought that triggered the emotion.

Feelings can be changed through acceptance, shifting perspective, and choosing different thoughts. Another key part of the **Thought–Feeling–Action–Result** chain is beliefs—a belief can trigger a thought. When you uncover the belief, it becomes much easier to break the cycle.

For example, let's say you experience worry when you feel stuck on a task at work. That worry quickly escalates into fear and anxiety, and suddenly, you feel the urge to grab chips to calm down and continue functioning. This reaction may be fueled by a thought like:

> *"I'm worried my boss will notice I'm struggling and fire me. We have so many bills to pay. We might end up relying on food banks, losing our house, and becoming homeless. My kids' future will be ruined."*

At this moment, eating chips becomes a distraction from those painful thoughts and emotions.

This process happens so quickly that you need to train yourself to notice it. You'll be amazed once you start catching yourself in these patterns. Here's the solution:

- If you want better results, you need to modify your actions.
- If you want to change your actions, you need to cultivate more positive emotions.
- If you want positive emotions, you need to choose better thoughts.

CHOOSE BETTER THOUGHTS TO CREATE BETTER RESULTS

Your thoughts are based on your self-image and reinforce it. The automatic mind seeks confirmation of the old and familiar, constantly looking for proof of its existing beliefs because it finds safety in the known. In doing so, it supports old programming by noticing evidence that reinforces familiar beliefs. This is how a self-fulfilling prophecy is created. The automatic mind sees what it believes to be true—and reinforces the belief.

Have you ever noticed annoying, repetitive thoughts? They stem from old programming and might trigger self-sabotage to keep things the same:

- *I hate doing this.*
- *I'm not the kind of person who succeeds at this.*
- *This is way too complicated for my brain and level of education. I don't have the patience for this. I don't have time for this. This is too hard.*

These self-sabotaging thoughts are old and familiar, and you might have believed them for years. When your automatic mind is in control, it provides "evidence" that these thoughts are the only truth. If you leave automatic thoughts unchecked, they will continue to trigger the same negative feelings, leading to unwanted actions and unhelpful results.

You need an open mind to become aware of automatic thoughts and a willingness to prove them wrong. The automatic mind will often send them your way when your willpower is challenged. You don't need to believe every thought that arises.

You don't even need to argue with them—just release them. Every time an unhelpful thought surfaces—such as: *This is never going to work for me*—change it with an empowering mantra: *Everything is always working out for me.*

Choosing a different thought may seem difficult at first, but with practice, you will strengthen new neural pathways, and this action will become part of your new self-image—your new automatic habit.

You are an amazingly powerful co-creator of your reality. Because what you think, you attract more of. You tend to get more of whatever you focus on. Remember Baader-Meinhof—the frequency illusion: our brain will always deliver confirmation of our thoughts.

Catch those thoughts:

- *I am not the person who does [insert things you want to do].*
- *Things never work out for me.*
- *I am weak.*
- *I am lazy.*
- *I am never going to lose weight.*

Your brain will discard any confirmation of the opposite and will focus on the thoughts you most frequently think. In a later chapter, I will explain how to plant evidence that the opposite about you is true. For now, simply catching yourself and deliberately choosing a different thought is enough.

This is the Law of Attraction: like attracts like. Our Universe is pure energy. People are also energy.

People create an energetic frequency with their thoughts. Feelings are how people describe the frequency they are in. Like attracts like. The Universe generously sends more of whatever vibration people are in. That is the meaning of "What you believe is what you receive" or "Thoughts become things."

How people show up every day—starting with their thoughts, the ideas they express through words, the judgments they make, and the way they perceive situations—affects how the Universe responds to their vibration. In this way, people are co-creating the reality they experience daily.

You get to choose your thoughts and co-create your life the way you want it to be. You may not believe this to be the case, but it is true all the same.

You need to be conscious and deliberate with your thoughts. Thoughts are powerful forces of creation. The more you obsess about something, the stronger it becomes. As you know, some thoughts have been repeated so many times that they have become automatic—a part of a bad habit. But they can still be changed. Your feelings will indicate when you are going in the wrong direction with your thoughts. As soon as negative, unsupportive, or unproductive thoughts arise on autopilot, put a big red X over them and move into neutrality. You need to start deliberately choosing your thoughts to create the body and health you want and to build the life of your dreams. If you don't control your thoughts or update your programming, your old mindset will take over automatically. Your thinking will remain on autopilot. You will think the same thoughts you usually think, feel the same emotions you usually feel, take the same actions you usually take, and get the same results you have now.

Just like growing a garden, if you want to cultivate beautiful, healthy plants, you need to plant the right seeds, water them, fertilize them, and pull out the weeds. Only then will you have a thriving garden that brings you satisfaction. If you do nothing, weeds will take over.

The same applies to your mind. If you allow habitual thinking to prevail, you will continue to get the same results you have right now. You become what you think about. To change our results, we must change our thoughts at the root cause—our programming.

One of the best ways to control our thoughts is to recognize when the Mean Voice starts talking in our heads and replace its negative comments with new statements or affirmations.

When I look back at the years when I binged, I realize I did it every time something good was happening. This was my form of self-sabotage. I was bingeing to fill the black hole. That black hole started with negative comments about my appearance or my ability to handle a situation. Doubts would rise up, expand into worst-case scenarios, and spiral into paralyzing fear.

At a certain point, when I couldn't take the mental torture anymore, I would eat—a lot. There were times when I resisted food but gave in to spending every penny I had, shopping uncontrollably, trying to close the black hole. But the addictive behavior always started with a negative comment bubbling into my mind. I had to learn to recognize when my "Mean Voice" started talking, distinguish it from my own voice, and stop taking its slurs seriously. Please use the Mean Voice Worksheet to stop the attack in its tracks.

To access the
Mean Voice Worksheet

SCAN THE QR CODE:

SCAN ME

THE MEAN VOICE

The Mean Voice fuels our perceived limits so that we stay exactly where we are and never step outside of our comfort zone.

Some of the things the Mean Voice says would be considered bullying if you were to say it out loud. If you would never say things like that to a friend or a child, you have to stop the Mean Voice from saying them to you.

Here is a three-step exercise that you can use to start taking back control from your Mean Voice.

1: Name It

This helps you recognize when it starts speaking and to distinguish it from your helpful voices. What name would you like to give to your Mean Voice?

_____

_____

2: Recognize Its "Slurs"

Notice the judgmental, negative slurs that are coming from your Mean Voice, then question them rather than accepting them as the truth. These are usually around things that are particularly important to you, and those you are particularly sensitive about—your appearance, your finances, your relationships, your career, your home, etc.
Mean Voice Slurs Examples: "You look fat" or "Don't even try, you're never going to be able to do that."
Identify your Mean Voice's Slurs:

1. _____ 2. _____

3. _____ 4. _____

5. _____ 6. _____

7. _____ 8. _____

9. _____ 10. _____

3: Change Your Mean Voice Slurs into Affirmations:

Do not try to reason with the Mean Voice. That is a battle you will always lose, because it will argue for your limitations, confirming them. Instead, call it out for what it is, ignore its commentary, show some empathy for its clumsy attempts to protect you from the scary unknown, and quickly insert the antidote against its poison.

When I think of my own Mean Voice, I often remember my grand-mother, who screamed when she was afraid for us. My grandmother, God bless her soul, was trying to protect us by using the only method she knew, to call us names as loud as she could.

Example:

Mean Voice: "You look fat"
You: "I hear you, Devil. And what you're saying is nothing

more than one of your slurs. I know that you're trying to keep me safe by blocking me from feeling confident and beautiful. Feeling confident and beautiful is safe for me. Thank you for looking out for me."

There's a universal law of the opposite: dark-light, inside-outside, negative-positive. That means that whenever you hear a negative commentary from the Mean Voice, choose the opposite from the affirmations below:

AFFIRMATIONS

Pick those that feel good for you and you can believe in, or make up some of your own:

1. Everything is always working out for me.
2. Every cell in my body vibrates with health.
3. I have unique gifts and talents that are needed.
4. I am patient and loving with myself.
5. Every day, I am becoming stronger and healthier.
6. All that I need is already here.
7. I choose whole, healthy foods as an act of love for myself.
8. I am surrounded by people who love, respect, and support me.
9. I give myself permission to change.
10. There are no limits to what I can achieve.
11. I am protected, supported, and loved by the infinite power of the Universe.
12. I am open to receiving everything that I can imagine.
13. I look forward to changing and embracing my new lifestyle as it unfolds before me.
14. My body and I are deeply connected and in tune.
15. As long as I'm moving forward, I cannot fail; I can only learn and grow.
16. I love and respect every single cell in my body.
17. I am worthy of the success coming my way.
18. I make compassionate choices toward myself.
19. I know that whatever happens, I am safe.

20. The Universe is conspiring in every moment to bring me happiness and peace.

Affirmations are a great way to update the subconscious programming. An affirmation is a statement that relates to the *feeling* and your vision of yourself:

- I choose the best for my body, mind, and soul.
- My potential is limitless.
- I always choose how I feel.

There are two rules for the effectiveness of the affirmations:

1. You need to feel really good when you repeat them,
2. It needs to be a statement that you believe. If your affirmation is too far away from your reality, it might create more stress. Scale down to what feels true.

Create an affirmation that is positive and closer to your current truth, make sure it feels really good in your body. Repeat it to yourself as an antidote to worry, doubt, Mean Voice's slurs, fears, insecurities, and judgments.

If it feels right, you can set up an everyday trigger for your affirmation, such as washing your hands or driving. When it's time to wash your hands or start driving, repeat your affirmation in your mind.

We learn by repetition. Please be patient with your Mean Voice, as you need to repeat your affirmations against its negative slurs a hundred times when you are starting this work. But believe me, the new sense of freedom and mastery is worth every second of your time.

In the space of letting go, let it all be, feel the smile coming over your face, feel the light breeze blow the weight away from you, and enjoy becoming the best version of you...

KEY POINTS:

1. The Dopamine Trap can be avoided by engaging in feel-good activities.

2. Mindset Programming (use the Limiting Statements Worksheet): Let go of your judgments, excuses, regrets, living in the past, blame... learn to make decisions quickly to go forward toward your goal.
3. Accept your fears: Growth happens through a battle with homeostasis.
4. Learn how to make decisions.
5. Let go of limiting beliefs, statements, and doubts to surge to the next level.
6. Mean Voice: Use the Mean Voice Worksheet to distinguish it from your own voice.
7. Use affirmations to counteract the Mean Voice slurs.

Pillar 3:

Acting from the New Self-Image

CHAPTER 4
YOU ARE NOT YOUR AUTOMATIC MIND

"Nothing can stop the man with the right mental attitude from achieving his goal; nothing on earth can help the man with the wrong mental attitude."
– Thomas Jefferson

If you want to break old habits, you need to break old neural pathways. But you cannot change what you cannot see, so first, you need to get out of autopilot to pinpoint exactly what needs to be changed. That means practicing mindfulness at every opportunity. In this chapter, I share tools that can help you stay awake and aware.

THE MIRACLE OF PERCEPTION

Aaron decided it was time to start feeling better, so he stopped drinking beer every day. After the first two weeks, he commented on how great he felt—his energy was increasing, he didn't feel sleepy in the afternoon, and he didn't miss beer at all. He even started exercising because he felt like it. And then, on Friday night, he had six bottles of beer while watching hockey. The next day was brutal. Aaron spent all of Saturday recovering in bed. When he told me why he felt so bad, I asked, "Why did you decide to drink beer if you already had proof that it doesn't make you feel good?"

"Because it was Friday, and I deserved it after my busy week," Aaron answered.

Beware of that little voice in your head that whispers, "I deserve it" or "I'm tired. I've had such a busy week, and I have an even busier one ahead. I've been so good all week—I deserve this treat. I'm going for it!"

This is self-sabotage talking. It makes people believe that the food they are trying to avoid is a treat and a form of self-care.

Let's look at a new perspective on what a "treat" really means. "I deserve this" implies that this treat is a gift to yourself—something really great.

Unfortunately, in our society, what is considered a treat—food or drink—is often a harmful substance. The big food industry has strategically positioned and promoted these items as treats.

For example, chocolate—which often contains harmful high-fructose corn syrup—has been marketed as a substitute for an intimate relationship. But what really happens when you eat it on an empty stomach?

- It spikes blood sugar, forcing the pancreas to pump out insulin to stabilize it.
- The adrenal glands must work harder to balance the sugar influx.
- If you're stressed or sleep-deprived, excess sugar further exhausts the adrenals. Sugar suppresses the immune system, increasing inflammation throughout the body, tissues, and joints.
- The liver must break down excess fructose instead of focusing on processing hormonal metabolites. The spike in stress hormones throughout the brain and body can mimic a panic attack—especially when paired with caffeine.

Does that sound like a gift of love—or torture and self-abuse?

Next time you hear that little voice whisper, *"I deserve it,"* take it as a signal to stop and ask yourself:

- What do I really deserve? What do I actually want? What would I prefer instead?

Maybe you're tired and deserve a nap. Or maybe you'd love a gorgeous, juicy fruit salad. Or a short session of gentle yoga with restorative poses. Or a good laugh over the phone with your best friend. Or cuddling with your kids, partner, or pet. Or a walk in nature to reconnect with yourself, to hear what you truly need.

Change your perspective on what a treat means, and ask yourself what you truly deserve. And maybe what you need is actually self-care.

I see self-care as a service to the people around me. Because when I take time for self-care, I become the best version of myself, full of energy—for me and for the people I love.

Why is this so important when you're working to transform old habits and patterns? Remember, your brain is wired to avoid pain and seek pleasure. When you feel hungry, angry, lonely, tired, exhausted, overwhelmed, or completely depleted, your brain perceives this as pain.

And what does your brain want you to do to avoid pain?

To go on a reward-seeking mission. This behavior is automatic, so you go straight toward the old, unhelpful habits and patterns you are trying to avoid repeating. This can include food, alcohol, TV, social media, etc.

A more effective way to prevent these moments of low energy is through regular self-care—engaging in activities that boost feel-good hormones such as endorphins, serotonin, and oxytocin.

The following are common signs that you're not making self-care a priority:

- You feel exhausted but have difficulty falling or staying asleep.
- You wake up tired in the morning.
- You look forward to food, alcohol, TV, or social media as a reward at the end of almost every day.
- You struggle to motivate yourself to move your body.

- You feel lonely and disconnected—from yourself and from something greater. (Whatever that means for you: the Universe, Divine Energy, Mother Nature, God, Source of Energy, etc.)
- External stimuli, such as the demands and opinions of others or deadlines, can easily throw you off track.

Sometimes, people confuse self-care with personal hygiene, pedicures, manicures, or massages. While those are nice, true self-care is about connection—first, within yourself (mind, body, and soul), and second, with a Power Greater Than Yourself. When we lack these connections, we often feel anxious, overwhelmed, lonely, worried, stressed, angry, or afraid—and we end up reacting to life on autopilot.

CO-CREATING WITH A POWER GREATER THAN YOURSELF

Becoming deliberate about the changes you want to make is key! When you're on autopilot, you automatically think the same thoughts, do the same things, and get the same results. You react to people, places, and circumstances the same way you always have—constantly trying to catch the daily curveballs life throws at you.

This leaves you feeling stressed and exhausted from trying to keep up with life's demands. In many cases, coping with stress leads to overeating, mindless eating, or choosing unhealthy foods. You may unconsciously repeat the same self-sabotaging habits—racing for ice cream and potato chips just to stop feeling bad. This is a perpetual vicious cycle you need to break.

In this chapter, I share specific strategies that I use to help you break free from autopilot, become more intentional with your thoughts and behaviors, and cultivate healthier habits.

Here's your gift of awareness: once you understand what's happening, you can change it. The problem is that most of us live in a constant state of reaction. But you have the ability to become the creator of your thoughts, your feelings, and your actions. And when you do that, you become the co-creator of your day—and your life.

One of the biggest obstacles to co-creating your own reality is not trusting that your Power Greater Than Yourself always conspires to bring you the best circumstances for your growth and to meet your needs. Once you start trusting your Power Greater Than Yourself, you begin to feel that you are always in the right place at the right time.

If you are engaging in compulsive or self-destructive behavior, it likely means that you, too, have a growing black hole inside. No amount of distractions or pretending "I'm fine" will fill that void.

Your Power Greater Than Yourself is the only antidote.

Unhealthy behaviors are often a sublimation of your soul's cry for help. Your homeostasis will present excellent arguments for why you can't change. But turning toward the omniscient Power Greater Than Yourself can serve as much-needed evidence against sneaky homeostasis.

Our minds create stress by trying to control everything—attempting to manipulate external circumstances without addressing the root cause of their creation. This is a form of self-sabotage that can leave us exhausted and send us right back to the starting point.

We cannot control other people. But we can learn to control our emotions—and by doing so, we influence the emotions of those around us through mirror neurons.

We can't control life. But we can co-create our future. Just like we don't entirely control our heartbeat, yet we can make it race by imagining a worst-case scenario, or slow it down by choosing calming thoughts.

On a side note, I'm happy that we don't control all bodily functions. Imagine if you had to consciously perform digestion—going out to eat lunch and then needing to close the door to your office, sit down, and focus on digesting for an hour and a half. Imagine how many people would be walking around with undigested breakfasts, lunches, and dinners!

"I'm sorry, I can't join you for dinner tonight—I didn't have a chance to digest last night's meal."

We influence our digestion by slowing down when we sit down to eat instead of eating on the go. We co-create with our bodies.

I am convinced that it's a good thing we don't have to consciously control many bodily functions—we just have to act on a cue. Thirsty? Have a glass of water. Hungry? Have a snack. Tired? Take a nap.

The more we try to control people and events around us, the more life becomes unmanageable, and eventually, we burn out. Co-creation of our reality begins with trust—trust that everything will work itself out in the best way possible.

You have probably seen many times how events unfold in a way that is just perfect for everyone involved. But you can only connect the dots when looking back. You could never have predicted how events would unravel, so there is no need to grip tightly and try to control everything and everyone.

When you step into your power as the co-creator of your own life, you feel less stressed and less overwhelmed. You gain better control over your impulses and become less vulnerable to the food cravings you once used to manage stress, overwhelm, and other uncomfortable emotions.

Effective self-care means deliberately choosing activities that align you with the Power Greater Than Yourself and your true self. This is recharging.

A pedicure is a form of personal hygiene that makes people feel good about their appearance. But it doesn't foster deep connection and alignment. You need to take time to connect with the source and recharge your battery. Otherwise, you risk feeling physically and mentally drained, leading to willpower fatigue. Neuroscience confirms that the more distracted, tired, or anxious people are, the less activity there is in the brain's self-control systems.

When people feel mentally, physically, or spiritually run down, they switch to autopilot, and old habits and patterns get triggered. Additionally, when people feel disconnected from the Power Greater Than Themselves, as well as from their own body, mind, and soul, they become easily distracted from their true path by external factors—other people, situations, deadlines, or unexpected events.

This is when people find themselves:

- eating a colleague's birthday cake, forgetting they were staying away from sugar;
- skipping a workout because of a work deadline;
- getting drunk after a fight with their partner.

They are not connected to the source. They forget what is *essential* and *make* the *circumstantial the essential.* They are not aligned. And they are easily thrown off course.

When you remain the center of your own Universe and make self-care a priority, practicing a deep sense of connection to your Power Greater Than Yourself and your body-mind-soul, you can weather any storm life throws at you.

Your power comes from the source. You act with clarity and make strong, wise choices.

You respond instead of reacting.

You become almost impossible to manipulate.

And you become a beacon for others.

I consider self-care a non-negotiable practice. Here's what it might look like:

MEDITATION

Life is our school. It offers many hidden lessons. Conditioned by their fears and expectations, many people never learn to cope with life.

People's minds are constantly spinning, endlessly searching for distractions from reality, trying to escape constant change, unavoidable death, looking for meanings and a big purpose, wanting safety, demanding certainty and pleasure, trying to understand the mystery of life.

When most people dream big, they get bitter and confused because reality never matches their dreams. They search for happiness, which always feels just around the corner—but they never turn the corner.

Turn off your automatic mind.

- Your mind, not other people or external circumstances, is the source of your moods. Here's what usually happens in our minds: We have to deal with things we don't want—and that makes us suffer.
- We don't get what we want fast enough—so we suffer.
- Even when we do get exactly what we want, we suffer terribly —because we fear that we won't be able to hold on to it forever.

Our automatic mind can be our predicament. It wants freedom from responsibility, pain, change, and death. While change and death are laws of life, no amount of postponing responsibilities or pretending we will live forever will set us free from suffering.

It's not life that makes you suffer—your mind does. Stress happens when your mind resists what is and creates judgments about it. To enjoy the ride freely—no matter what happens—you must alter your mindset, accept change as a law, and co-create your future.

Meditation doesn't turn off your brain or wipe your thoughts away. Instead, it allows you to observe your thoughts as they arise, shifting you into the role of the Observer. You are not your thoughts. You can see yourself thinking. You can choose and change your thoughts. You are not your feelings. You are not your judgments. You are not your limiting beliefs. You are not your fears. This is incredibly empowering! It means you have the power to choose who you are, choose your thoughts, your beliefs, and your actions. You are the creator of your thoughts, your emotions, and your actions. And as a result, you are the co-creator of your life.

That is the miracle of perception. You can choose to perceive every situation in your life differently. You are the Universe. As within, so without. Beneath your thoughts and feelings, there is the *knowing that All is always well.*

You start to see your worries and stresses as something you can turn off. You become aware of your subconscious programming. And you can change what you can see. You can actively become the best version of yourself.

Meditation is the most powerful tool for awareness and mindfulness. It is a workout to break free from autopilot and strengthen your mindfulness muscle. Even just two minutes of stillness—focusing on your breath, bringing your wandering attention back—can make a difference.

Meditation engages the prefrontal cortex, the center of rational thinking and self-control.

For all these reasons, meditation is an essential tool to strengthen mindfulness and shape a better version of yourself.

MEDITATION IS AN EXCELLENT TOOL TO COMBAT STRESS

The Ohio State University Medical Center found that more than 170 genes are affected by stress—especially due to chronic cortisol secretion—with hundreds shutting off completely, including those responsible for wound healing, inflammation, sleep, metabolism, and cardiac function.

A meditation study examined twenty volunteers over eight weeks of meditation and yoga. At the end of the study:

- 1,561 genes were changed in novice meditators.
- 874 genes were upregulated for health.
- 687 genes were downregulated for stress.
- Blood pressure was lowered.
- Heart rate improved.

In experienced meditators, 2,209 new genes were expressed—most of them improving health and body response to psychological stress. There's no supplement that can do that. This is unreal.

Use the Meditation Handout to help you make meditation a daily practice. You can also explore various meditation apps.

To access the
Meditation Handout

SCAN THE QR CODE:

SCAN ME

JOURNALING AS SELF-CARE

Journaling is a task that engages the analytical and rational left brain, allowing the right brain to create, "download" insights, and feel. While your left brain is occupied, your subconscious mind unlocks deeper parts of yourself—offering clarity, understanding, and new perspectives on your life, others, and the world around you.

Journaling is a way to connect with yourself and with the Power Greater Than Yourself. It can give you clarity, insight, motivation, and momentum to stay consistent in your new healthy lifestyle. Some people use journaling to "download" messages from their higher self or to develop their intuition. When people understand that intuition always has their best interest at heart, and they learn to trust this voice, even the most difficult situations unfold in the best possible way—beyond their imagination.

Writing down your feelings and thoughts can help reduce stress, manage anxiety, and help cope with depression, as shown by numerous psychological studies. It also helps you process trauma and pain. You can also use journaling to express and process uncomfortable emotions, rather than avoiding them through unhealthy habits and patterns around food. Journaling allows you to dig beneath the surface, explore emotions in a private, safe, and controlled way, and heal—without using food as a coping mechanism.

Journaling cultivates self-awareness by helping you identify incongruences in your life, gain clarity, and notice things you might otherwise miss. Journaling also helps you clarify your goals, work through confusion, pinpoint challenges that are holding you back, recognize where you're self-sabotaging, and uncover solutions you might not otherwise see. Sometimes, people feel stuck while trying to reach big goals. When you journal regularly, you "unload" your thoughts onto paper, allowing you to discover answers and solutions from a new perspective. Journaling also helps you track progress toward your goals.

Journaling can also highlight a tendency to focus on the negative while fostering hope. If you only see where you've failed or where you're stuck and seem to ignore your improvements, writing down all the choices you've made that you are proud of on a regular basis can help you shift perspective. By doing so, you begin to redefine what you're capable of and who you are based on actual evidence rather than your brain's assumptions and automatic thinking. You're using your memory, reasoning, and perception, leaving your brain no choice but to recognize that you are becoming the best version of yourself.

Often, people learn new skills and tools to build a healthier relationship with food, yet never fully integrate them into their lives. Journaling helps reinforce learning by allowing you to capture new ideas and tools—from books, podcasts, articles, and blog posts—and figure out how to apply them in your daily life.

You can also use journaling to reinforce affirmations by writing out a particular affirmation you're working with five or ten times a day.

HOW TO START JOURNALING

There are many different journaling approaches, styles, and prompts you can explore. Use the Journaling Handout to decide which journaling approach works best for you. Give it a chance—pick one method, sit down each day with pen and paper, and commit to it for three weeks to experience how this tool can help change your mindset.

To access the
Journaling Handout

SCAN THE QR CODE:

SCAN ME

Some other examples of self-care include:

- Sleep, prayer, contemplation, laughter, reading, time in nature, and spending time with loved ones.
- Spending time with animals.
- Eating a clean, nutrient-dense diet, cooking, and baking.
- Energy work (Theta healing, Reiki, etc.).
- Service to others.
- Moving your body—exercising, yoga, triathlons, walking, dancing, hiking, etc.
- Visiting art galleries, museums, the theater, listening to music.

- Engaging in creative activities—painting, writing, singing, knitting, etc.

MASLOW'S HIERARCHY OF NEEDS

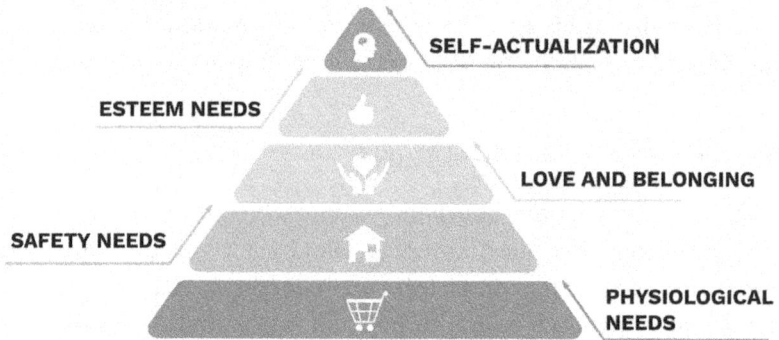

If you look at Maslow's Hierarchy of Needs, you'll see that physiological needs are at the base, followed by safety, love and belonging, then achievement (esteem), and finally, self-actualization—reaching one's full potential, including creative activities.

Some people never take the time to understand what brings them joy. Many believe they should wait until retirement to enjoy these activities, which often leads to a life that feels unfulfilled—one they never truly get to experience. You need to find what makes you happy —and do more of that.

Ask yourself:

- *What activities make me feel recharged and alive?*
- *What brings me joy or makes me feel most like myself?*
- *What makes me feel connected to my higher self?*
- *What do I always wish I had more time for?*

Then, do lots of that.

Give your new self-care routine a three-week trial before dismissing it. Do not get caught up in the "shoulds." Don't force yourself to do something you don't enjoy just because you think you should like it.

Start trusting yourself and listening to what your inner voice is telling you. What you need today may not be what you need tomorrow. Some days, I need to listen to live music. Other days, I need to immerse myself in beauty—so I schedule museum trips.

In the next chapter, I will share how to effectively schedule serotonin-boosting activities.

FALL IN LOVE WITH YOURSELF

Connection to your Power Greater Than Yourself, meditation, journaling, and the self-care activities I've mentioned all boost feel-good hormones—serotonin, endorphins, and oxytocin. These feel-good activities are essential if you want to reach your goal. They help create the necessary balance of neurotransmitters so that your brain shifts from obsessing over food, weight loss, work, shopping, etc., to mindfulness and experiencing the bliss of everyday life lived with purpose. I strongly believe that feel-good activities should be scheduled into your daily routine. I will give you the exact planning blueprint to help you reach your goals without setbacks and avoid burnout.

When people hear about the importance of self-care, they resolve to incorporate it into their "to-do" list as just another item to check off. And then they never find the time—because, deep inside, they don't truly believe that self-care is a priority.

I suggest putting self-care on your to-do list because you truly, deeply believe that you are worthy. Because you respect your soul, appreciate your body, and want only the very best for yourself. But making time for self-care requires self-love.

All healthy habits—such as eating whole foods, exercising regularly, maintaining a morning routine, meditating, ending negative self-talk, setting boundaries, etc.—require self-love.

The struggle to find time for self-care is real. It comes from putting everyone else's needs before your own. You wouldn't deny a child in your care sleep, good food, creative play, fresh air, time with friends, or cuddles. Your body, mind, and soul are the child in your care. Love yourself enough to make self-care non-negotiable—an automatic priority. This is your reason. Because you love yourself, and you deserve love—and all good things. Love will fuel your consistency in maintaining a healthy lifestyle.

HOW DO YOU FALL IN LOVE WITH YOURSELF?

Use the same steps you would take to nurture love in a relationship with another person. The same components—such as quality time, respect, generosity, gifts, communication, trust, integrity, fun, honesty, and compassion—apply to your relationship with yourself.

Listen to your soul, heart, and body. Pay attention to struggles, resistance, and what helps you thrive. If it's been a long time since you've opened these lines of communication, you may need to get used to the subtle messages they are sending you. Turn inward and listen to what's happening inside you every day.

Trust your intuition. Your body and heart know what's best. Honor and respect them by making self-care and reaching your dreams a priority.

Set aside time for activities that help you feel your best, such as sleep, movement, spiritual practice, and the things you absolutely love to do.

Treat yourself with gifts that are truly good for you.

Cancel the blame game and take responsibility for your life, finances, health, and relationships.

Stop talking to yourself in a way you would never talk to a child or a friend. I once went on a date with a guy who started commenting on my weight. He was out in five minutes. I want to be admired— honestly, I do. So I don't take sh*t from anybody.

But I also don't say bad things to myself. I have learned to look for the best when I stand in front of a mirror.

Be honest with yourself—uncover the excuses that are stopping you from making healthier choices and living your best life.

Keep your word when you make promises to yourself. Simply do what you say you're going to do.

You probably have an example of a person with integrity in your life, who keeps their word, and you know you can trust them. When someone promises to do something and doesn't keep their word, they lose your trust. It doesn't feel good to be with someone who's dishonest and makes excuses for broken promises and bad behavior. They let you down, they don't take responsibility for their actions, and it hurts. You don't want to allow people like that in your life. Because they break your trust, they break your heart. The same applies to yourself. If you keep telling yourself you're going to eat better, exercise more, or prioritize self-care—but keep breaking those promises—you are treating yourself without integrity.

Over time, this chips away at the trust you have for yourself. Your self-esteem plunges. It takes a toll on your soul.

You stop trusting yourself. You stop liking yourself. You don't even want to be with yourself—the person who lacks integrity. You don't feel good about yourself. And then, your limbic system might send you searching for rewards—to numb those feelings. Like overeating.

And then, a piece of cake looks like the only thing that can save the day right now.

After eating that cake, people feel guilt and remorse for breaking a promise to themselves. That nagging thought creeps in: "I am bad. I feel bad. Why did I do that?" And the vicious cycle continues.

So, how can we become congruent? How can we start doing the things we know we need to do and stop sabotaging our best efforts?

Stop breaking your own heart. You know, it feels good to act with integrity.

If you make promises to yourself, keep them. Start with baby steps. Keep one simple promise to yourself just for today—such as going for a short walk after lunch. And then, just DO IT.

Then, register how it feels when you do that. Take some time to just feel it. You kept a promise and acted with integrity. You feel in control, proud of yourself, strong. FEEL that. Absorb it. Enjoy it. This way, you are teaching your brain to pay attention and find evidence that you are becoming the best version of yourself.

That is how you apply the same elements that form a healthy relationship with another person to create a healthy relationship with yourself. My coach, Hina Khan, once said, "You cannot be betrayed if you don't betray yourself first." How profound is that? We show people around us how to treat us the way we treat ourselves.

This is the only way to foster self-love. It starts to grow in your heart and affects your thoughts, beliefs, and actions—with PRACTICE.

Practice every day. Self-love is a practice.

Ask yourself sporadically throughout the day: What would I want?

What would I prefer? What would be great? What is the most loving act I can do for myself?

KEY POINTS:

1. Use every opportunity to practice mindfulness to switch your mind from autopilot.
2. Changing your perception creates miracles in everyday life.
3. Practicing regular self-care prevents setbacks.
4. Co-creation with a Power Greater Than Yourself puts you back in the driver's seat.
5. Meditation helps to switch from autopilot and allows controlled thoughts.
6. Journaling is a great way to connect to self, reflect, and channel your highest self.
7. Showing up for yourself with integrity is the way to create respect and self-love.

CHAPTER 5
PLANNING FOR SUCCESS

"You do create your own reality. No one else does."
– Jerry and Ester Hicks

IMPLEMENTATION INTENTION

In a 2018 article published in *Psychology & Health*, researchers in Boston sought to help busy people aged 35 to 69 find time to exercise. Participants were given a pedometer and divided into two groups.

The first group—the so-called control group—was asked to simply track how much they walked each day.

The second group received specific instructions to plan how, where, and when they would incorporate additional steps into their daily routine to meet their step goals. They were provided with personalized schedules and maps.

The second group showed significant improvements in:

- Number of steps taken
- Time spent in moderate-to-vigorous activity
- Time-relevant exercise self-efficacy (confidence in their ability to fit exercise into their schedule)

Participants who achieved their goals reported:

- Greater confidence in their ability to exercise despite time constraints
- More positive emotions on a daily basis

These findings suggest that a personalized planning intervention can effectively increase physical activity levels and boost confidence in achieving exercise goals, even for people with limited time.

I think you know what I will ask you to do now. Yes! You guessed it. Use the version of you that achieved your goal as a reference. In the present tense, list three implementation intentions for the activities that this self does in the course of one week.

1.

_____

_____

_____

_____

(*Example: I have my balanced breakfast at 6:30 a.m. at home Monday through Friday, alternating between a gluten-free porridge and scrambled eggs with gluten-free toast. For lunch, I eat my balanced salad that I bring from home in the break room at 12 p.m. I have my balanced dinner at home at 6:30 p.m., alternating between a stew and a stir-fry.*)

2.

_____

_____

_____

_____

(Example: *I do a weight-lifting session at the gym with a personal trainer at 5 p.m. on Monday, Wednesday, and Friday.*)

3.

_____

_____

_____

_____

(Example: *I go for a 20-minute walk to feel the sun on my skin at work after lunch at 1 p.m. Monday through Friday.*

Now, it ALL COMES TOGETHER. You have your exciting goal that connects the logical and emotional parts of your brain. You have updated your internal self-image and created the best version of yourself—one that has already achieved your goal. You have listed three implementation intentions for the whole week to bring you closer to your goal.

Do you see what I mean when I say that once you master this strategy for goal achievement, you will become unstoppable? Now, we need to schedule these activities in your planner because as soon as you start taking these steps, you start achieving your goal.

When a goal feels too far away, it may seem irrelevant, and you might lose motivation. The farther away your goal feels, the less motivated you may become.

That's why the next step is to break your goal down into three-month and one-month segments.

Running 100 meters feels much shorter than a marathon. The closer the goal, the more excitement you feel.

Now, let's get into planning. For the purpose of planning for success, your month consists of three weeks of dedicating 10% of your time to your goal, and one week of observation and adjustment.

You have your big, juicy dream goal—one that completely challenges your homeostasis. To avoid self-sabotage (in the form of procrastination, perfectionism, etc.) and stay motivated, we need to break the big goal into bite-sized goals.

Carefully choose three behaviors that you want to adopt within one month (e.g., thinking positively, moving your body daily, being present with your partner, etc.), and use the Planning–Monitoring for Success Worksheets to self-coach and track your progress.

To access the
Planning-Monitoring for Success
Worksheets

SCAN THE QR CODE:

SCAN ME

My biggest challenge in planning is limiting the number of actions I want to work on. I usually want to change everything all at once. It's like asking a three-year-old to make a list of presents for Santa: "I want a new puppy, a castle, an elephant ride, a snow fort, ice cream, lots of candy and cookies, a life-sized stuffed lion, a real lion, a robot, a diamond crown, a small car I can drive myself everywhere, and all my relatives and friends to live with us!"

So, I plan to work on—improving my communication with my husband, building two business platforms in two languages at the same time, spending more time with my daughter, exercising seven days a week, cooking from scratch, removing the clutter in the basement, discarding old files in my office, clearing my wardrobe of outdated clothes, networking and writing my next book... Are you getting dizzy just reading it? Yes!

As you already know, planning to change more than 10%–15% of your daily activities can be a form of self-sabotage because it will definitely alarm your homeostasis. Choose a maximum of three activities that harness the power of your brain by stimulating different parts of it —activities you will concentrate on improving or changing each month:

1. Fundamental habit (focused on overall well-being)
2. Dopamine-stimulating habit (something exciting that boosts motivation)
3. Feel-good, self-care habit (something enjoyable and restorative)

If you master just one fundamental habit per month, you will have changed 12 habits by the end of the year. In this case, going slower will actually make you unstoppable.

The main habit should be fundamental—focused on systematic care for your overall health and well-being.

This could include:

- Changing your diet
- Consistent physical activity
- Mental health care
- Improving your sleep

Choose one fundamental habit for one month.

The second habit should be dopamine-stimulating—something that excites you and elevates your self-image.

This could be:

- Learning a new skill
- Building a new relationship
- Trying a new form of exercise

Essentially, this should be something that pushes you out of your comfort zone.

The third habit should be a form of self-care—something that you already know how to do and enjoy. This could be:

- Drawing
- Reading poetry
- Cooking
- Spending time with friends (e.g., playing board games at the end of the week)

- Getting a massage
- Being intimate with your partner (A hint for my single readers: a good massage elevates oxytocin levels!)
- Daily walks

All three of these activities shouldn't take more than 10–15 hours a week to keep homeostasis at bay. We all have around 100 waking hours in a week. 10%–15% of that is 10–15 hours, which is the time needed to implement these three activities into your week.

We need to alternate dopamine-stimulating activities with feel-good activities to maintain a balance between motivation, work, and pleasurable activities. The feel-good activities are non-negotiable because these two to three hours a week can prevent you from slipping into obsession about reaching your goal "right this immediate second," protect you from burnout, and stop you from white-knuckling through the process.

Here's an example of how you can integrate three activities into 10–15 hours a week:

- **Fundamental project: Prepping your food:** 1 hour on Sunday, plus 30 minutes every day – 4.5 hours
- **Serotonin activity: Weights-lifting training or Taekwondo or salsa dancing:** 1.5 hours 3 times a week – 4.5 hours
- **Dopamine activity: A daily 20-minute walk in nature or a date with your partner (sex, dinner)** – 3 hours

These activities can be implemented even during a very busy time.

SUCCESS POINTS TO CHECK

Your plan should be very clear. The human brain avoids uncertainty because it perceives it as scary and painful. The more unclear the task, the more effort it takes to get started. Vague plans add to confusion and lead to self-sabotage. The human brain prefers clarity. For example, instead of writing *"meal prep for 30 minutes,"* go over your meal prep guide and write down exactly what you need to do: *"Cook the Lentil Masala soup. Cut vegetables, portion them with hummus dip, and store them in the fridge."* Or, if you're working on building consistency in your workouts, label them in your calendar as *"Workout 1,"* *"Workout 2,"* and so on, instead of vaguely writing *"Workout."* I know—it might sound counterproductive to describe each task in detail, but doing so raises the likelihood that your brain won't avoid them.

Make sure that your fundamental and dopamine tasks last no longer than 30–90 minutes at a time. A duration of 30–90 minutes is the sweet spot for our brain to complete an activity. Anything beyond 90 minutes feels too much, and the brain may shift into procrastination mode to avoid hard work.

Budget your time as realistically as possible. Estimate the exact time required to complete a task. For example, if your workout lasts 90 minutes, your schedule should also include travel time to the gym, changing into workout clothes, a shower after the workout, and getting dressed again. These extra steps add about 30 extra minutes, which must be factored into your planning.

To catch a monkey, people make a hole in a box just big enough for the monkey's paw and put a banana inside. When the monkey reaches in, it can pull its paw out—as long as it doesn't grab the banana. If it grabs the banana, its paw gets stuck in the box, and the monkey cannot escape. I'm not calling you a monkey, but you need to release your bananas to avoid getting trapped in self-sabotage. If, after writing down exactly what you need to do to complete the fundamental task, you find that the timeline is extending beyond 10–15% of your available time, scale down your tasks.

Consider buying pre-cut vegetables, ordering meal prep services, or scaling down your dopamine activity. Don't attempt to do the tasks faster—this will create overwhelm and exhaustion, which feel like pain and lead to self-sabotage. Your brain prefers being poised over being rushed. Don't skip your feel-good activity to make extra time for the fundamental or dopamine task. If you do, you may end up self-sabotaging first and burning out later, because your brain needs to feel rewarded for its hard work.

Block time for your tasks in your calendar. Your brain thrives on knowing what's coming next. Of course, life is unpredictable, and you may need to reschedule some tasks. But you are far more likely to complete them when you have a clear task, an exact timeframe, and a designated slot in your schedule.

MAKE TIME FOR FEEL-GOOD ACTIVITIES

"I'm too busy! I get the idea of making time for self-care and feel-good activities, but I just don't have time," Christine told me.

"What do you enjoy doing?" I asked.

"I like to draw, and I do it sometimes. But not right now," answered Christine.

She came to see me because she had gained significant weight, started feeling lethargic and apathetic, and was losing interest in activities she had previously enjoyed. I considered Christine's medical diagnoses of diabetes, high blood pressure, rheumatoid arthritis, fibromyalgia, etc., and suggested she follow an autoimmune paleo (AIP) diet to help relieve the pain and stiffness in her joints, lose weight, and regain energy.

Three weeks on the autoimmune paleo diet produced great results: Christine lost 20 pounds, her energy level went from 5 to 9, she could walk without pain, and she felt happier.

Being a retiree, Christine had developed habits that made living alone enjoyable. She tried to take the best care of herself. As soon as Christine started feeling more energetic, she took on more social activities. She loved helping people, so she became a companion to an elderly woman in a retirement home and visited her every Monday. Christine drove her friend for chemotherapy treatments every Tuesday. Every Wednesday, she had coffee with a friend. She had dinner with her brother every Thursday to keep him company after his wife passed away. She went to brunch with friends every Saturday. And Sunday was the day of her mental health support group.

Christine was sure she would follow the AIP diet until she lost all her excess weight to feel better. That was her goal. But on our next call, she told me that because she was too tired to meal prep, she switched back to her "usual" pre-AIP grocery shopping and ate the foods she was supposed to avoid. As a result, within a week, Christine couldn't leave her apartment due to an arthritis and fibromyalgia flare-up. Now, it was really hard for her to take care of herself. This is how self-sabotage shows up in people's lives to save them. Christine ignored self-care, didn't schedule her feel-good activities, and became too busy with external demands. She increased the time spent helping others by 70%. Her self-sabotage showed up as going back to safe and familiar foods, even though they were highly inflammatory.

Self-sabotage had to make it painful for Christine to move, forcing her to stop all her activities and take time to recover. This is why it is so important to stay within 10%–15% of new activities and include feel-good activities to avoid burnout and self-sabotage. You don't find time —you plan your feel-good activities to ensure your brain feels rewarded and continues supporting new lifestyle changes.

Self-care must be one of your top priorities for your mental health. If you are serious about transforming your body, health, and life, feel-good activities should be scheduled in your calendar. This gives you evidence that you are thriving, not merely surviving the fast pace of modern life. Otherwise, your automatic mind will take over, your old coping mechanisms will be activated, and you might even burn out completely. You simply cannot afford not to schedule your feel-good activities.

It would be strange to hear someone say, "Personal hygiene is great, and I know other people find time to shower every day, but I just don't have time to do it." Even busy people make time to shower because, in this culture, it is a non-negotiable priority.

Self-care is part of your service to the people around you. When you take time for self-care, you become the best version of yourself. You and the people you care about deserve your best version.

To schedule time for self-care, you need to create boundaries. Your energy, time, and focus are limited. When you say "yes" to everything —to doing things that will make others happy—you often take this time away from your feel-good activities. This cuts off the connection between your mind, body, and soul or your Power Greater Than Yourself.

You need clarity about your priorities to help you determine what to say "yes" to and what to say "no" to.

Ask yourself: What are the top three priorities in your life right now? Once you've identified them, you can plan them out and work on them over the next three months. Your priorities will likely change over time. What is important for you today? Being present for your partner? Spending more quality time with your kids? Getting a massage? Drawing?

You will be able to have them all over time, but maybe not all at once. You must pick one that is going to be your priority for the next month.

Once you've picked one, you have your decision. Anything that directly brings you more success in this area is a "yes," and everything else is a "no." In the last chapter, I will share how to say no and create more time in your day.

MORNING ROUTINE

If you want to make sure that you start every morning on the right foot, with your brain switched to the prefrontal cortex, a morning routine can help ensure that. From the moment you open your eyes in the morning, you can behave deliberately and mindfully instead of reactively and habitually. A morning routine is an ancient technique that has been used by people seeking enlightenment. You don't have to wake up at 3 a.m. and chant for two hours. Your morning routine activity can take anywhere from 5 to 20 minutes and set the tone for the whole day. Please use the Morning Routine Handout to choose an activity that will help put your conscious mind in charge of your behavior right from the start.

To access the
Morning Routine Handout

SCAN THE QR CODE:

SCAN ME

A morning routine is a series of practices that you do upon waking to switch your brain into mindfulness and firmly take back control of your day.

Usually, when people feel grumpy and overwhelmed at the start of the day, they assume the worst and try to manage all the chaos that only gets crazier by the minute. By 9 p.m., they are completely exhausted and end up eating highly processed foods in an attempt to switch off stress mode.

You can take back control of your thoughts, feelings, and actions as soon as you wake up and co-create the best possible day, feeling satisfied, calm, and successful in the evening. There are a number of different elements I have described in the Morning Routine handout that you can try. I suggest experimenting with different elements and then using two or three that feel best for you to start your day.

I believe that writing down your big goal every morning, reading it out loud, and then visualizing yourself achieving it can plant your goal and vision in your subconscious, ensuring that you stay on course toward achieving it.

These daily repetitions will help you imprint the new version of yourself into your subconscious mind. Are you ready to reach the next level where you feel and look your best? Seeing is believing. See yourself achieving your goal. Get used to the fact that you are healthy, beautiful, slim, sexy, feeling amazing, and looking great.

Before starting your day, you can also do a five-minute check-in to see where you stand with your activities and course-correct right away.

What does my morning routine look like?

- Water
- Prayer
- Coffee
- Writing my goal
- Visualization
- Study & Exercise

My morning routine puts me in a powerful state so that before lunch, I have usually completed my most important tasks for the day, feel proud of myself, and still have plenty of energy left to enjoy and create the best day ever—every day.

If you would like to join my morning routine, send me an email at info@irinacazazaeva.com.

REPETITION

Your brain doesn't create new wiring around a thought or behavior just because you have it or do it once. You must repeat it over and over and over again in order for those neurons to fire together enough that they eventually wire together. This is why we learn by repetition.

Whether it's deliberately choosing empowering thoughts, meditation, or visualization, we reprogram our subconscious mind through repetition, just as people learn any new skill through repeated practice.

The key here is to recognize and accept that, as you build these new neural pathways that will eventually form the foundation of your new identity, it might feel hard, awkward, and tiring. That's your old neural pathways breaking apart and new ones forming. Don't give up! It will get easier.

Repetition helps to imprint our intentions in our unconscious mind. The CPD Certification Service (the world's largest independent Continuing Professional Development accreditation organization) emphasizes the importance in an article on their website: "Repetition sounds simple enough, but it requires a high level of patience. When stimuli are learned by repetition, they are remembered better and retained for a longer time. Studies have shown that the brain forms new pathways when a task is repeated often, thereby optimizing the performance of the skill."

VISUALIZATION

What do Fortune 500 CEOs, Olympic athletes, and Academy Award-winning actors have in common? They practice visualization of their achievements before they become reality. Visualization is a regular practice of imagining yourself as the person you want to be, thereby shifting the trajectory of your life by allowing your mind to expand beyond the limitations of homeostasis.

By imagining that you have already reached your goal, you condition your mind to bring you evidence of possibilities for your vision. Feeling the emotions that come with achieving your goal puts you in alignment with its vibration. Using the language of the Law of Attraction, visualization helps raise your energetic vibration—starting with your thoughts and then your feelings—allowing you to "tune in" to the energy of what you want to experience in your life.

For example, if your goal is to have a healthy relationship with food, how do you approach food once you have achieved it? What foods do you enjoy? Do you like to cook? Do you order food? What do you order? How do you eat? How do you feel in situations that might trigger old habits? What choices do you make? How does it feel to embody your goal? How does it feel to be in the body of the person who has already achieved it?

You can tap into visualization by journaling—writing down all the best-case scenarios that feel uncertain. Don't allow your judgments, fears, outdated beliefs, or resistance to block your imagination. Do not let your rational mind interfere by asking, *How do I get to the goal?* because the "how" is a homeostasis trap. Just don't go there. You are not meant to predict the future. However, chances are, if you feel calm and eat healthily today, you will feel calm and eat healthily tomorrow. Allow your imagination to describe the best-case scenario without worrying about the how. The how will reveal itself one step at a time as you move along your journey. Imagine you have already succeeded at all of it. What does that success look like in your life? How does it feel to be there? Spend some time evoking those feelings.

People's brains easily believe that what they imagine is real. When people watch a scary movie, they feel scared. When people take placebo pills, they experience the placebo effect. The subconscious mind doesn't know the difference between reality and imagination; it does not recognize time or distance. A strong childhood memory can trigger the same thoughts, emotions, and hormones as if it were happening now.

You can harness the power of visualization to your advantage and make your brain believe that what you desire has already happened.

When you practice, on a daily basis, visualizing yourself as the person who has already reached your goal, your brain grows new neural pathways around these thoughts, feelings, and beliefs, automating the process through repetition.

This phenomenon helps you make choices based on your new identity, making being the new you feel natural and automatic.

You already use visualization all the time—when you wake up in the morning and imagine how the day ahead will unfold. You might worry about a deadline at work and immediately feel stressed, anxious, or overwhelmed. Visualization works when your worries trigger automatic catastrophizing, worst-case scenarios, and imaginary arguments with people in your head.

It takes me 30 seconds to start a fight in my head and create a horror movie. And then I feel my blood pumping, my breathing becoming faster, and my anger rising.

"My life is full of tragedies that never happen, thank God!"

You visualize your vacation during a boring day at work. You imagine how nice it will be, and you feel excited and happy.

You think about having a difficult conversation with someone or going to a party. Without even realizing it, you are setting up expectations in your imagination—deciding in advance how you think those experiences will go, including what will happen and how you will feel.

You need to use visualization to your advantage and imagine the best-case scenario, where everything you want is already here. Use that power to focus on what you want: this will help you achieve your goal.

WHAT VISUALIZATION CAN DO FOR YOU

Visualization can help change your self-image. What kind of person do you think you are? What do you believe you are capable of? As my peak performance mindset coach, Hina Khan, likes to say: "Most people are defending a false identity." If you have the awareness that your self-image is limiting and holding you back, use visualization to reshape it. You can imagine a situation you currently find challenging —such as coming home after a busy day—and change it in a way that works best for you. Imagine yourself in that moment, feeling exactly what you wish you could think, feel, and do. With regular practice, you will begin to see yourself differently, and you will start acting like a different person.

You can train your brain to resist temptations by imagining exactly how you say, *No, thank you. I don't go for seconds when I'm no longer hungry.* Or, *I am the person who doesn't cancel a workout because of a deadline.* When you visualize this situation multiple times, you won't experience an internal tug-of-war when it happens in reality.

So, let's talk about how to visualize yourself achieving your big goal. Imagine you have just reached your goal. Use the questions below to visualize it in vivid detail. Picture yourself doing something that symbolizes success. Maybe it's getting dressed in the morning and feeling gorgeous in everything you put on, driving through the drive-thru with your colleagues and only ordering a cup of coffee, or feeling strong through vigorous training. The key is to see from inside yourself —hearing and *feeling that situation happening.*

Answer these questions:

- Where are you?
- What are you doing?
- How does it feel to be in your body?
- What are you wearing?
- What do you see?
- What do you hear?
- What do you smell?
- Who else is there?
- What's going on around you?
- How do you feel when you accomplish your goal? Happy, excited, proud, free?
- How do other people feel about you?

Once you've imagined yourself inside your goal vision, write it down, say it out loud, and take a couple of deep breaths, releasing and letting go of judgment and everything else. Close your eyes and see yourself in your goal—experiencing it fully through your own eyes. Shut off your inner critic and enjoy being there.

Repeat this process daily: write your goal, say it out loud as if you believe in it, and visualize it. The more you practice, the more your mind will generate powerful details and emotions in your vision.

Eventually, you will want to create a vision for every aspect of your life once you experience how the power of visualization shapes your reality.

KEY POINTS:

1. Write down your implementation intentions to reach your goal.
2. Use planning for success: write down your foundational activity, write down your dopamine activity, and write down your feel-good activity.
3. Make sure to check the success points.
4. Make time for self-care to avoid burnout.
5. Start a morning routine to connect to your goal every day.
6. Our brain gets re-wired through repetition.
7. Visualization is one of the fastest ways to override the homeostasis.

Pillar 4:

Manifesting Evidence of the New Self-Image

CHAPTER 6
YOUR CONFIDENCE IS RISING

"Man's main task in life is to give birth to himself,
to become what he potentially is."
– Erich Fromm

MONITOR YOUR ENERGY TO AVOID BURNOUT AND SETBACKS

You've created a beautiful plan for success. Now, to avoid setbacks and burnout, you need to monitor your energy to make sure that you are in the three most productive conscious states 80% of your waking time.

I wrote extensively about self-care and feel-good activities in the previous chapter to give you resources to take care of your energy. Being in a productive state is the most important task for you and for people you care about. The following table presents the full spectrum of conscious states, from the most distressed state to the most burnt-out state, with the three most productive states of mind in the middle.

Monitor Your Energy		
State of Distress	**State of Productivity**	**State of Burnout**
Panic, Anxiety: automatic behavior, can't concentrate on anything but the subject of panic, wrong state for making decisions, can "go bananas"	**Interest, Commitment:** conscious behavior, a very productive state	**Lack of Energy:** detachment, passiveness, automatic behavior due to a lack of energy
Agitation, Worry, Unease: automatic behavior, brain's energy is draining in the attention of the worry, beware of snappiness	**Balance, Stability:** conscious behavior, the best state for creativity, making decisions, control	**Burnout, Apathy, Insensibility, Stupor, Inability to act:** automatic behavior, tired and wired, can't relax, can't sleep, can't do anything new, no brain power
	Relaxation, Calm: conscious behavior, this is the after-meditation state, when the attention is clear and ready to be directed to the desired subject	

As you can see, only in the three most productive states in the middle are you in complete control of your behavior.

Take five minutes to use the Planning–Monitoring for Success Worksheets to monitor your state of mind every evening. This will help you identify when you are going into automatic behavior in the early stages, and this lowers the intensity and the duration of the setbacks. The ultimate goal of this monitoring is to review the worksheets during the Observation Week, discard the tactics that lead to setbacks, and create a low-maintenance lifestyle that keeps you in a stress-resistant mode 80% of the time.

REPLACE JUDGMENT WITH CURIOSITY

Remember what you learned earlier about your brain's primary focus: avoid pain, seek pleasure, and conserve energy. The brain registers any form of physical or emotional discomfort as pain, and instinctively pivots away from it toward something safe and familiar.

Sometimes, we can't avoid pain or stress. However, you can use certain tools to become stress-resistant and handle life's challenges without setbacks. You can start by scaling down the additional pain you might be causing yourself and steering clear of triggers that lead to automatic food-seeking behavior.

Often, when people make a mistake—whether it's choosing French fries instead of a salad or skipping a training session—they beat themselves up for an eternity.

In Buddhism, there is a poetic parable about the poisoned arrow. When a man wounded by a poisoned arrow was brought to a doctor, instead of allowing the doctor to treat him immediately, the man started asking questions: "Who shot the arrow? What kind of arrow is it? Did it come from our village or the neighboring village?" As the doctor tried to answer all of these questions, instead of pulling out the arrow and administering the antidote, the man died from the poison.

Your "arrow" is the mistake—the wrong choice of food or the missed training session. Your poison is the way you react to the mistake—your self-inflicted judgment day. Your brain registers judgment and self-blame as excruciating pain and automatically shuts down willpower, pushing you toward immediate pleasure-seeking behavior, such as food. You don't need to poison yourself.

Here's what you can do: take a deep breath, replace judgment with curiosity, review what happened, and change your perspective. When you shift your perspective to gratitude, the experience transforms. You have already made this mistake, so now you know how it feels. By examining why it happened, you gain the knowledge to prevent it in the future. This frees you from judgment and allows you to let go.

For example, you went out for lunch at your usual spot with colleagues and automatically ordered French fries instead of a salad. That is the arrow.

You were so hungry and immersed in the conversation that you only realized afterward that you broke your commitment to yourself.

Here, you need to step out of automatic behavior. Instead of judging yourself harshly, beating yourself up, and allowing the poison to spread—leading to a downward spiral and more food-seeking behavior—put a big red X on judgment and get curious. Imagine this as a science project where your goal is to understand what triggered your choice.

You are not a bad or weak person for ordering fries. Now that this automatic behavior has surfaced, you need to figure out how to prevent it from happening again.

BEHAVIOR REVIEW

This process helps you develop more positive thoughts that generate more pleasant feelings, which then fuel better actions—helping you move toward your big goal. When you become aware of an automatic behavior that goes against your goal, conduct a Behavior Review to pinpoint the thoughts that led to it. If you only focus on the action without uncovering the root cause—the thought—the behavior will continue to repeat itself.

It would be very helpful to remind yourself that this habit originated with a thought, which triggered a feeling, which then led to an action. The entire habit structure has been repeated so many times that you ordered those fries automatically without even thinking twice.

Think back to what you felt at the restaurant when you were there with your colleagues. Get curious about the feelings that triggered your unwanted behavior.

On a physical level, you were hungry.

On the emotional level, you were excited to have lunch with colleagues. You all ordered the same—a burger and fries—because you always eat a burger and fries at this restaurant, and you didn't feel like bringing attention to yourself by ordering a salad instead of fries. You wanted to fit in. You avoided looking different from your group.

Now, go to the belief that is at the core of: *I don't want to attract attention because I order something different.* Here, you might be afraid of being judged by your colleagues. *If I order a salad instead of fries, they might not invite me to have lunch with them*—or even worse, *If I lose the weight, they will call me the skinny bitch, and I will become an outcast of this group.*

With the root thought identified, it's time to challenge it with some questions:

- Is it a fact, or is it my opinion?
- How do I feel, and what do I do when I believe this?
- How would I feel, and what would I do if I believed the opposite?

Here's how this would look in the context of the example we've used above:

- The feeling is fear, and the thought behind it is, *I will become an outcast of this group.* You are an adult. Why is being an outcast a problem? Why is it a problem that people think you're different? *"Because that means they don't respect me.* Why is that a problem? *I don't deserve respect.*

You found your root thought. Now, let's challenge it.

- Is it a fact, or is it your opinion that if others don't respect you, you don't deserve respect? *How do I feel, and what do I do when I believe that if others don't respect me, I don't deserve respect? —I feel fear and stress.*
- *How would I feel, and what would I do without this thought? How would I feel, and what would I do if I believed the opposite? What if what other people think of me didn't matter?*

This process is laid out for you in the Behavior Review Worksheet.

To access the
Behavior Review Worksheet

SCAN THE QR CODE:

SCAN ME

RECOGNIZE YOUR TRUE COMMITMENT

I need to let you know about an interesting psychological oddity that arises when our mind is lying to us... again. We often confuse obsessing about something with taking action on it. Our minds imagine that because we've been reading, researching, and *thinking* about doing something new, we're actually taking action.

Manifestation of the New Self-Image Evidence Tracking helps us see the distinction between *thinking* about change and *actually* doing it. It can give us the motivation we need to start acting instead of just contemplating.

The Manifestation of the New Self-Image Evidence Tracking is an excellent tool for recognizing your current level of action in any area you've decided to change.

PERFECTIONISM

"Better is the enemy of good."
– Voltaire

One word of caution against perfectionism. As you know, perfectionism is a form of self-sabotage—to demand perfection is to set impossible expectations, leading to inevitable failure. Expecting to eat 100% natural, high-quality food without any deviations from your meal plan and follow your longevity lifestyle to the letter can backfire with painful self-judgment. This is exactly what happened in Yasmina's story when she planned to eat two squares of chocolate but ended up eating the whole bar before she could stop herself. She thought, *I ruined my diet…* and, in response, overate even more.

If you allow yourself to just do your best for today, over time, doing your best will become easier and better.

If your goal is to eat healthily consistently, allow yourself to eat 80% of the food that is good for your body chemistry and leave up to 20% for daily adjustments. Doing your everyday best will make some days look like 98% "healthy food," while other, more stressful days might be closer to 60%–70%. Hold on to the positive.

For example, if your only real and honest choice for dinner is pizza, count it as a carb, add a protein that you have access to, and include a small salad if possible. If protein and salad aren't available, then simply make your next meal as healthy as possible—and let it go at that.

This is what doing your best today looks like. By allowing yourself some flexibility, you are not giving yourself a reason to feel guilty.

Use Manifestation of the New Self-Image Evidence Tracking—it helps you see your progress, shows your honest commitment, and gives you visual evidence of the manifestation of your new self.

Your self-image is based on your beliefs about yourself, which are then confirmed by your actions. If you avoid physical activity, you might say, "I am not very sporty." But which came first? The belief or the evidence? The more you believe in your old self-image, the more evidence you will see to reinforce it, and the stronger the core belief becomes.

My mom cooked a lot, but I was never interested in cooking when I was growing up. In fact, I considered myself a terrible cook based on 1.5 failed attempts at making eggs and cooking a complex soup. When I moved to Italy by myself, I learned how to make a salad and boil pasta—which was, honestly, a huge step forward for my cooking skills.

I actually became interested in cooking at 33, when my husband and I got tired of takeout and going out every night just to find something to eat. I discovered that I love cooking—it's my feel-good activity. At 47, I even earned a culinary certificate. I am a good cook now, especially when I follow the recipe…

My husband started cooking at 42 after I showed him the miracle of scrambled eggs. Now, he's one of the best cooks I know. He cooks everything. I mean, we eat a variety of delicious dishes every day. That's how much people can change when they let go of their old self-image and the limiting beliefs that come with it.

Life experiences and lifestyle modify your self-image. The more you repeat certain actions, the more evidence you create of doing them. You can become the new version of yourself by repeating the actions that the person who achieved your goal would do.

HOW TO MANIFEST THE EVIDENCE OF THE NEW SELF-IMAGE

As you learned, there are many ways our brain deceives us. Plus, our brain likes to be right, and it will find confirmation of old self-image beliefs and present them as truth. Your brain will show you a million pieces of evidence that you haven't changed a bit and never will, all in an attempt to keep you in your comfort zone.

Chloe said, "I love sweets. I can't live without sweets. I will never lose weight because I can't stop eating sweets."

She couldn't help believing her brain. Her grandma told Chloe that she had a sweet tooth, and she reinforced that belief by always choosing sweets, which messed up her blood sugar and drove her to eat even more sweets. Now, Chloe's belief about her sugar addiction was supported by the evidence of her behavior.

Sugar, fat, shopping, gambling, social media, and even the pursuit of love can become dopamine traps. That's another reason why it's so hard to stop eating candy and chips before the bag is empty.

Your brain defends old limiting beliefs and restricts your self-image to fit inside the box of your old story. It finds all the evidence to support the old belief and old life story while discounting anything that contradicts it. This is how limiting beliefs end up running your life.

If your goal is to lose weight, and in your previous attempts, you struggled to stay away from certain foods, you may have constructed statements such as, *I'm weak, I have no willpower,* or *I'll never be able to lose weight.* When you repeat that thought enough times, it becomes a belief, and your brain—always wanting to be right—focuses only on evidence that supports the belief while ignoring or dismissing any proof to the contrary. For example, *I ate a bagel. I have no willpower. I can't lose weight!*

Once Chloe started eating balanced meals, she discovered that she could skip a sugary treat. It was especially easy to avoid sweets when her blood sugar was stable, which gave her an emotional boost—proving that, with proper nutrition, she was not behaving like a sugar addict.

Chloe made sure to eliminate all foods that triggered her sugar cravings from her environment and wrote down every instance when she chose a balanced snack instead. Her small daily wins accumulated into a full month of evidence that she could avoid her once "favorite" sweets.

Seeing the evidence on paper became the manifestation of her new self-image—one her brain finally accepted as the new truth—which made her confidence soar. This is why I included "writing down your wins" in the Planning–Monitoring for Success Worksheet.

To access the
Planning-Monitoring for Success
Worksheet

SCAN THE QR CODE:

SCAN ME

I find it logical to write down your wins in the Planning–Monitoring for Success Worksheet. You can see what you planned to work on this month and track your achievements on the way to your big goal. You can also carry a small notebook with you or record a note on your phone to track every single piece of evidence that you are the new version of yourself—such as choosing healthy food, going to bed on time, or showing up for your training session.

When you want a second helping but take a moment to connect with your body, realize that you are almost full, and skip it—or even just put a small portion on your plate—write it down as a win.

When you choose lemon juice and olive oil dressing instead of ranch, write it down as a win.

When someone brings a cake into your office, and you avoid the break room to resist temptation, write it down as a win.

At the end of the week, review all the points of the Manifestation of the New Self-Image Evidence in your tracking.

When you see the evidence written down in front of you—that you've successfully avoided sugar multiple times throughout the day, chosen healthy foods every day, and exercised—you start appreciating how strong your willpower actually is, and your confidence grows.

When you use tracking to notice your wins and take the time to show your brain the evidence of your new behavior, it allows you to override your brain's attempt to diminish and ignore the manifestation of your new self-image. This simple tool helps you see that the old limiting beliefs and old stories you once held about yourself belong to your past self. You can also use this evidence against your Mean Voice's slurs.

When you consistently and determinedly use the Planning–Monitoring for Success Worksheet, you will be amazed—and maybe even shocked—at how quickly you are manifesting your new self-image. Sometimes, this is the only way to compel your brain to see that the old belief at the core of your past self-image ("I'm someone who is addicted to sugar") is no longer valid. This is how neuroplasticity rewires your brain to work in your favor.

Take 15 minutes for the **End of the Week Reflection:**

1. What did I achieve in my fundamental habit?

---

2. What did I achieve in my dopamine habit?

---

3. What did I achieve in my feel-good habit?

As I shared previously, my old self-image was really distorted. When I yo-yoed between restricting food and bingeing to calm myself down, I saw myself as weighing over 300 pounds when, in reality, I weighed 154 pounds. I also thought that if I allowed myself to eat when I was hungry, I would eat too much. When I tracked the amount of food I ate daily for a couple of weeks, I saw evidence that my appetite was normal. Plus, I saw that I chose whole, natural foods instead of processed ones. I was not what I thought of myself. Tracking helped me see the truth. Tracking helped me see the facts and showed that "I eat too much" was just my distorted opinion about my natural hunger.

OBSERVATION WEEK TO SUMMARIZE EACH MONTH

At the end of four weeks, allow yourself 30 minutes of observation to draw conclusions about what worked and how many manifestations of your new self-image you experienced during these four weeks. What is the main change? What did I do to change? How has my vision of myself changed this month? How can you improve each habit? Discard plans and actions that didn't work.

List the mistakes in a new way. Instead of beating yourself up for them, look at your mistakes as lessons. Failure and success are just ideas—the judgment gives them meaning. You simply tried to do an action in a certain way and got feedback on how to improve it. Do you see the new possibilities? This allows you to recognize where you might benefit from more intention toward bringing your goals and actions into better alignment.

And now, you can plan your next month. Please use the Planning–Monitoring for Success Worksheet to list the three new fundamental, dopamine, and feel-good habits you want to work on next month. Then, monitor your energy, track your commitment, and list your wins every day to see the evidence of the manifestation of your new self: *When I focus on what's bad, I have a bad day. When I focus on what's good, I have a good day.*

As bestselling self-help author Napoleon Hill put it, "Make up your mind—TODAY—to be happy! Only you have the power to do this, and it's easy if you know that the only difference between happy people and unhappy people is attitude."

I had to learn this lesson the hard way. In 2007, I was very close to committing suicide because I could not stand the self-inflicted torture of my life. On the outside, I could still pretend that everything was okay. On the inside, I could not take it anymore. I was suffering from clinical depression and took four to five antidepressants daily. I was also using food to cope and self-medicating with alcohol, which started as a glass of wine after work. I also took drugs at parties to fit in.

When I was looking to get better, I quit smoking cigarettes and quit party drugs. But then, food and alcohol started to take over. By chance, I picked up the book *Undoing Depression* by Richard O'Connor, MD. This book showed me that, in order to stop myself from plunging into depression, I had to adjust my nutrition and lifestyle and remove all depressants, starting with alcohol. Then, I learned that I had to adjust my mindset.

I experienced trauma. I could write a whole chapter about my childhood memories of witnessing my father's and grandmother's battles with addiction—but I won't. I watched my mother lose a long fight with cancer. I was brainwashed by propaganda and became deeply skeptical and bitter when I discovered the truth. I witnessed the collapse of a great empire and the sudden rise of crime and violence. I lived through nationalism escalating into military conflict. I saw hope-lessness and anger in every adult's eyes as they lost their money, found themselves unemployed, struggled to feed their children for years, and fought to find their place in a new world.

I grew up in a culture of negativity, fear, and despair, where the most common belief was that everything was going from bad to worse at any moment, and we were to expect only suffering in this life. I had no idea that this paradigm almost killed me. You see, my constant expectation that the worst was about to happen created anxiety I could not tolerate. I used food and alcohol to calm down. The negative thoughts and catastrophizing were the real causes of my depression. I didn't need to overeat or drink alcohol to calm my anxiety. And gradu-ally, I didn't need antidepressants anymore.

All I needed to do was remove the depressants, adjust my lifestyle and nutrition, change my thought patterns, and engage in feel-good activities daily. This approach worked for me, but you might need a different one. If you are in a similar situation, consult and collaborate with your healthcare provider before considering going off antidepressants. Abruptly stopping antidepressants is very dangerous. Lowering the dosage should be approved by the doctor who prescribed your medication, and you should be monitored by your healthcare provider throughout the process.

Very gradually, I became a queen of gratitude and used all the tools I describe as self-care or feel-good activities. My depression left me. I still use all these tools and monitor my attitude every day. Because now, I love myself and consider this life a gift. I live in bonus years, where all my dreams are a reality. I want to live as long as possible while maintaining my amazing quality of life—this is my reason.

RESTART YOUR DAY AT ANY TIME

This little trick saved my marriage, improved my business relationships, and allowed me to wear my expensive Italian clothes from twenty-five years ago.

Everyone wakes up on the wrong foot or in a bad mood once in a while. You know, when the negative narrative inside your head becomes increasingly toxic with every passing minute. Before your moodiness attracts all kinds of fertilizer and life lessons you don't feel like learning all at once, restart your day. This might be the only effort you need to make before "moody" turns into batshit crazy.

When you feel like a victim, just stop, turn 360 degrees three times, or clap your hands three times, and make a quick 10-point gratitude list, like:

1. I am grateful that I woke up today.
2. Thanks for my health.
3. I am pain-free!
4. Thank you, Universe, that my husband is still here. (Don't mention that you wanted to kill him three seconds ago—let that part go for the sake of this exercise.)
5. Thank God for my healthy children. (Omit that argument about the dirty dishes that were not in the dishwasher, like you want them.)

6. I am so grateful for the cutest little furry friend that snores right now.
7. Thanks for the sunshine, which makes me feel alive today (or the rain, which makes me feel cozy).
8. I am grateful that I paid my bills.
9. Delicious coffee or tea or a glass of lemon water.
10. Hot water in the shower, a warm blanket, or a shady tree.

Whatever your situation is, you can find many things to be grateful for because you're still alive and probably got exactly what you needed.

Why do I suggest these seemingly pointless rituals? Restarting your day stops you from spiraling downward, creating chaos, and activating the pain avoidance mechanism in your limbic system, preventing behaviors like overeating, scrolling through social media instead of working, arguing, etc. The gratitude list is the quickest way to mentally reset, helping your prefrontal cortex take over again so you can continue your day on a high note.

CONNECT YOUR SUBCONSCIOUS AND YOUR HIGHER SELF TO CREATE YOUR REALITY

What people call synchronicity is actually the work of our mind—it brings us exactly what we are looking for.

I like to play a game: when I don't have an obvious answer, I ask my subconscious mind to show me the answer. I usually find it appearing in my inbox, through people around me, in a book, or through other media. Before falling asleep, you can ask your subconscious and your higher self to connect, bringing you answers or helping you create your desired reality.

With reality creation, it takes more time, but it will come—you just have to be patient and allow time for your desires to bring you the right people and circumstances. You must also persist. It's like going to a restaurant and allowing the chef to finish your meal. The more elaborate your order, the more time you need to allow for its creation.

This is where your determination comes in. Your order will be delivered—you just have to stay committed. Your life is not a microwave dinner. It takes time to bring you exactly what you want.

You can also change your order, but know that it will come with a delay. It's like ordering a roasted leg of lamb, which takes over 40 minutes to cook at a restaurant. If you change your mind after 30 minutes and order pasta instead, and then change your mind again, and then again and again, it will really delay what you originally asked for.

So, if you stated your goal and designed a new self-image that embodies your goal, give yourself time to change on a cellular level but stay determined to achieve it.

KEY POINTS

1. Monitor your energy to avoid burnout and setbacks.
2. Replace judgment with curiosity to neutralize the situation.
3. Review your behavior.
4. Recognize your true commitment.
5. Kill your perfectionism.
6. Collect the evidence of the manifestation of your new self-image to raise your confidence.
7. Track your actions.
8. Conduct the end of the week 15-minute-long plan correction.
9. Allow 30 minutes for integration week each month.
10. Neutralize your judgment about failure.
11. Restart your day at any time.
12. Connect your subconscious to create your reality.
13. Show yourself determination.

CHAPTER 7
REINFORCE NEW YOU

"Do not bite at the bait of pleasure,
till you know there is no hook beneath it."
– Thomas Jefferson

TEMPTATIONS

When Carlo decided it was time to quit smoking, he used hypnotherapy, which helped him stay away from cigarettes for two years. Then he fell in love with a girl who smoked, but he managed to resist the temptation to join her for several months—until they went on vacation.

Carlo's girlfriend invited her friend to fly out with them. During a fabulous Caribbean vacation, the three of them had a great time together. One night, while they were out drinking and dancing on the beach, the girls went to the bathroom and jokingly left Carlo guarding their lit cigarettes in both hands. In response to their joke, Carlo started smoking both cigarettes at once. It took just three seconds of staring at the burning cigarettes for drunk Carlo to start smoking again. When he returned from vacation, Carlo announced to everyone who asked why he had started smoking again that hypnotherapy didn't work.

CHANGE YOUR ENVIRONMENT

You've probably heard the saying that you are the average of the five people you spend the most time with. If you want to become a different person, you need to change your environment. Seek out people, places, and experiences that align with the person you want to be. This doesn't mean you need to abandon your family and move to Bali, but start actively seeking out events, retreats, podcasts, books, groups, and individuals that support your new self-image. One of the reasons 12-step programs work is that people let go of old relationships with those who trigger unwanted behaviors and start forming new relationships, attending social gatherings together, eliminating feelings of loneliness, making time to absorb the new knowledge, reflecting on it, and acting on it as part of their regular routine.

Don't provoke your bad habits. You don't need to make things harder for yourself or rely solely on willpower to resist the foods you've decided not to eat. Instead, make it difficult to indulge in unhealthy food. Remove from your home all the foods you tend to overeat. Do a kitchen cleanup when your willpower is especially strong—for example, set a two-minute timer on a Sunday morning right after breakfast and get rid of tempting foods.

DELAY DISCOUNTING YOUR TEMPTATIONS

Your brain favors instant gratification—"I want what I want, a lot of it, and right away." This mechanism is known in psychology as "delay discounting." It means that the further away a desired reward appears, whether in time or space, the less intense the desire becomes. The human brain evolved to seek immediate rewards for survival. A distant compensation—whether it's tomorrow or one hundred miles away—is considered less valuable by the brain.

On the other hand, the closer the temptation appears, the more attractive it is. That's why supermarkets strategically place medium-priced foods at eye level, while cheaper items are on lower shelves—forcing customers to put in more effort to reach them, making them seem less desirable.

You can use this knowledge to your advantage, especially when temptation is close by, by creating distance or delay between yourself and the object of your temptation—this allows you to shift control from your brain's reward system back to your conscious mind.

In the late 1960s and early 1970s, Stanford researchers conducted an experiment involving what has since come to be known as "the Marshmallow Test." Children were each given a marshmallow and told that if they didn't eat it for the next 10 minutes, they would receive two more marshmallows. Those who could delay gratification would double their reward. Then, the researchers left the room. Talk about cruelty! While many children caved immediately, some got creative in tricking their brains into waiting the full 10 minutes.

One child mentally framed the marshmallow as a picture, making it easier to trick his brain into believing it wasn't real. Another child used detachment techniques by placing the marshmallow outside his field of vision, turning away, and avoiding looking at it. These techniques increased the perceived distance of the reward, making it less tempting.

Neuroscientists confirmed that delaying the receipt of a desired object by 10 minutes transforms instant pleasure into a distant, almost irrelevant object, making an enormous difference in your brain's reward system.

Marina noticed that she gets a powerful craving for dessert when she is physically hungry. She knows that saying a flat "No" to herself when she's really hungry might backfire. So she gently says, "Sure, after you have a proper meal." Usually, after a balanced meal, her cravings are 0%–10% of their original intensity, so if she feels she no longer wants dessert, she skips it. If she still wants it, a small piece is satisfying. This is how Marina uses delay discounting and avoids eating too much sugar.

If you find that you are not physically hungry yet still tempted to eat something you want to avoid, try this tip: "I'll have it in 10 minutes." Set a timer on your watch or phone, remove the object of your desire from sight, and focus on something else you enjoy. You can also use the DARE technique (Describe, Accept, Review, and Exceed– we'll talk more about it later in the chapter) to uncover the hidden motive behind your craving.

You might discover that your craving has dropped to 20% of its original intensity once the 10 minutes are up. By allowing yourself to focus on something else, you have done an amazing job in neurocircuitry rewiring, changing the old pattern and its pathways.

ADAPT YOUR ENVIRONMENT TO YOUR NEW SELF-IMAGE

Make it easy for yourself to eat healthily. Promote healthy eating by placing the foods you are supposed to eat at eye level. Instead of candy, put a couple of fresh, washed apples or mandarins on a plate.

If you want to eat more whole foods instead of processed snacks, when you feel a craving to open a bag of chips, go into the kitchen and get a balanced snack that can satisfy your craving while containing protein, fat, fiber, and carbohydrates—such as sugar-free Greek yogurt and a piece of fruit. Of course, your food choices should be based on what is compatible with your body chemistry.

You also need to find a way to do the things you don't like in order to reach your goal—then form a habit of doing the things that "failures" avoid.

If you do not deliberately form good habits, you will unconsciously form bad ones. It's really easy to develop a habit of eating chips while watching TV because it requires no effort. Your mind is busy with what's happening on TV, and your taste receptors are entertained by highly addictive flavors made in the lab. Some of the greatest scientific minds were put to work creating addictive flavors, which is why it's so hard to put down that bag of chips, cookies, chocolate bars, ice cream, or soft drinks.

Similarly, brilliant creative minds were tasked with designing the most addictive TV shows. And you have to deliberately turn your TV off, or the series will continue playing automatically—you can't turn it off until the season is over.

Now, what about exercise, food prep, and grocery shopping? These are essential components of a healthy lifestyle. You must do these "boring" tasks to enjoy a great quality of life for as long as possible. Unfortunately, they aren't always fun, and they don't come anywhere close to the instant gratification of binge-watching TV or eating highly processed foods.

Now that we've established that these tasks are necessary, we need to find a way to do them even when we don't enjoy them. I hope that my own example of overcoming resistance to exercise can help.

By the age of nine, I had a belief that I was not made for exercise. It started when I was picked for a synchronized swimming team at age seven. When my mom was at work, my routine was to eat alone after school—whatever ready-made food I could find. Then I took one bus, transferred to another bus, and traveled for one hour each way. Then came two to three hours of training, including jogging, ballet, stretching, swimming, and synchronized swimming techniques such as hanging upside down in the water. The Olympic-sized pool our team trained in was outdoors, and I could feel the snow falling on my bare, wet skin. The cold temperatures, combined with long and intense training, demanded a lot of fuel, which I failed to provide for my body.

After learning about sports nutrition, I now know exactly what sabotaged my training sessions. I never took snacks with me and rarely had any pocket change to grab a bun and a bottle of milk at a food stand after training. So I was literally starving, and my body was breaking down my muscle proteins. Instead of experiencing muscle growth, I was wasting away.

After traveling for another hour, I got home. My mom heard me complaining almost daily about tremendous headaches and shaky hands and legs after synchro. *There must be something wrong with synchro or with the child,* she thought. She took me to a doctor, who diagnosed me with some kind of abnormal cranial pressure and wrote a note allowing me to skip gym class at school and quit synchro altogether. This is how I found myself sitting on the bench while my classmates played team sports.

Although the synchro training was tough, I liked it for a while. I showed enough potential and strength to become an elite athlete. But my brain made the connection between exercise and the uncomfortable hunger that followed. Thus, the belief "I hate to exercise" was born, and the doctor's diagnosis confirmed my conviction that I was not made for sports.

It took a lot of effort to start exercising again when I was a teenager. Now, I use the Suit Up & Show Up for Two Minutes method to fight resistance whenever it creeps in before a workout.

SUIT UP & SHOW UP FOR TWO MINUTES

It's 6:30 p.m. on January 20th. Outside, it's the proverbial "dead of winter"—pitch black, freezing cold, -19 °C (about 2 °F). I've just finished my after-dinner tea when I see a "Taekwondo" reminder pop up on my phone. Suddenly, a massive resistance attack kicks in. All kinds of thoughts flood my mind, reminding me how tired I must be:

My muscles still hurt from the cross-country skiing I overdid over the weekend. I conducted five client calls, followed up with paperwork, answered school emails for my daughter, and discussed the fireplace renovation with my husband. I feel like climbing under a warm blanket with a good book instead of changing into my Taekwondo dobok.

I feel this resistance almost every night before Taekwondo training, yet I never miss a session. I use the Suit Up & Show Up for Two Minutes, which I learned in a 12-step program.

For me, Taekwondo training doesn't start at the gym—it starts with brushing my teeth after dinner, putting on my dobok, preparing my water bottle, and driving to the gym. When I arrive and greet everyone, I feel better—because I'm keeping my promise to myself. Yet, even then, I still don't feel excited about starting the warm-up. So, I trick my brain: "I'll just do it for two minutes." I start my warm-up at a very comfortable pace, and soon, the master's voice and the energy of the group work their magic.

I stop looking at the clock and give 100% of my attention and effort to the workout. By the end of our 90-minute intense session—filled with kicking, jumping, punching, screaming, and pushing past my perceived physical limits—I feel amazing, as if I've just gone on a mini-vacation, thanks to the endorphins flowing through my body and the satisfaction of not betraying myself. Once again, I showed up with integrity, and Taekwondo goes into my "wins" section for the day.

The harder something feels, the more you might procrastinate. The easier it feels, the more likely you are to do it. If something takes less than two minutes, it feels doable and easy.

This is the essence of the Suit Up & Show Up for Two Minutes code. Your workout starts the moment you change into your workout clothes and tell yourself, "I'm just going to exercise for two minutes." Two minutes is the sweet spot for silencing your inner procrastinator.

At the end of those two minutes, you won't want to stop—because it already feels like you're in the middle of your workout, and you might as well finish it. Just don't go overboard if this is your very first workout. Increase intensity and duration gradually.

When you want to introduce a new habit and a feeling of massive resistance arises, if you announce to your brain that the task takes more than two minutes, it might appear too difficult for the brain to execute, and you might end up procrastinating. *I am just going to check my phone*, you think. And then, 30 minutes later, you realize you missed your training session because you were scrolling through social media.

You don't have to fight your resistance. You don't have to ignore it. Feel the resistance, accept it, promise yourself to check the phone after the training session, and do what you are supposed to do by taking just the first step and committing to doing it for the next two minutes.

That's how I prepare food when I don't feel like cooking. I put on my apron, set a two-minute timer, and do just one task. For example, I scrub a sweet potato, poke it with a knife, and put it in a pan, ready for roasting. Some days, two minutes are enough to finish a task. Other days, two minutes turn into 30, and I complete everything on my to-do list and still have the energy to do more.

The Suit Up & Show Up for Two Minutes code reinforces your new self-image. The more you repeat this process, the more neural pathways are created, making the habit easier and more automatic. When you Suit Up & Show Up for three training sessions in a row, you manifest the evidence of being your new self. Eventually, these new habits become automatic, and you see yourself as a person who doesn't miss training sessions and who exercises regularly.

You can use this method to establish any new habit in your lifestyle. Here are some examples of how you can use this method to create a low-effort healthy lifestyle:

- If you want to start jogging three days a week (Monday, Wednesday, Friday), change into your running clothes and jog or walk outside for two minutes. Gradually, you can add more minutes to your jogging or walking.
- If you want to visualize your goal consistently, every morning, while holding your coffee, write down your goal, say it out loud, and visualize it for two minutes.
- If you want to practice yoga regularly, set up your schedule, and when it's time, change into your yoga clothes, roll out your mat, and lie down in corpse pose for two minutes. Those two minutes might feel so refreshing that you decide to continue with a few more stretching poses.
- If you want to journal consistently, keep your journal near your bed and write just one sentence about your day as part of your bedtime routine.
- If you want to meditate daily, before going to bed, close your eyes, take ten deep belly breaths, and focus on your breath rising and falling.

The Suit Up & Show Up for Two Minutes method can help you build a low-effort healthy lifestyle, one habit at a time.

How can we make grocery shopping enjoyable? Start by having a grocery list with you and either ordering online (and repeating the order every other week for simplicity) or teaming up with a friend. Make it a fun friend date—after grocery shopping, go for coffee together. That way, it's no longer just boring grocery shopping—it's socializing with a friend.

Another necessity is meal prep. If you want to prepare healthy meals for the week, take two minutes on Sunday to look at your calendar, plan your meals, and write them down. I usually provide a meal prep guide with a meal plan. You can simply follow the step-by-step instructions on a Sunday morning after a great breakfast while listening to your favorite music.

ANNOYING DAILY TASKS AS SERVICE TO YOURSELF AND PEOPLE AROUND YOU

Here's another way of making a pact with your brain to do the difficult and unpleasant tasks you need to do to reach your goal: make them a way to care for yourself and the people you love, connecting to the highest universal good. This can turn tasks such as prepping food, washing the dishes, prepping the gym clothes in advance, or folding laundry into a form of meditation.

Instead of resenting it as just another chore you dislike and rushing to get it over with, be deliberate and change your perception of it from an imposition to a form of service. When you do these tasks in a mindful way, you cultivate a connection to yourself.

When you change your perception in this way, an annoying task becomes a form of self-care, and meal prep becomes spiritual work.

Don't forget about the power of gratitude when you speak of things that you have to do. Instead of saying, "I have to go grocery shopping," "I have to do meal prep," or "I have to go to the gym," you can say, "Today, I get to go grocery shopping," "Today I get to prepare my meals for the week," "Today I get to go to the gym." Because these actions bring the quality of your life to a whole new level, you get to take care of **yourself**. Do you feel the difference?

To summarise, you can use the Suit Up & Show Up for Two Minutes or reframe meal prep as a form of self-care—a service to yourself and your family, or even a spiritual connection to the highest universal good. Or, if there's no way you can enjoy meal prep, delegate it to a meal prep company or to a loved one who enjoys cooking.

IRONIC REBOUND

Imagine I asked you to do one simple task: Do *not* think of ice cream. What would you immediately think about?

In 1985, at Trinity University in Texas, psychologist Daniel Wegner conducted studies on thought suppression. He asked one group of students to avoid thinking about white bears. What the researchers discovered was that this seemingly simple task was almost impossible for the students.

The second group of students was asked to actively think about white bears. Ironically, the first group, who was told to suppress thoughts of white bears, ended up thinking about them more frequently than the second group.

Another interesting discovery was that the task became even more difficult for students who were distracted, tired, or stressed.

Wegner called this force "ironic rebound." When people try to force away a thought, it often returns with even greater persistence. The more people try to suppress the thought, the more strongly it rebounds, leading to an uncomfortable obsession over what they are trying to avoid.

Why is it so hard to make the human brain cooperate in avoiding a simple thought? Why, when told to eat fewer carbohydrates, do people suddenly obsess over how much they miss them?

When you try to avoid a thought, your automatic and conscious minds start working against each other. Your conscious mind focuses on avoiding the forbidden thought, while your automatic mind constantly checks for signs that you might be thinking about it.

As you probably recall, the automatic mind is highly energy-efficient, while the conscious mind requires a lot of energy to function. When people are relaxed and well-rested, these two parts of the mind work together smoothly.

However, when people are distracted, sleep-deprived, or stressed, their conscious mind begins to scale down in an effort to conserve energy. Meanwhile, their automatic mind keeps working at full capacity. In its attempt to ensure the thought is not present, the automatic mind paradoxically brings it up repeatedly.

This is why people struggle when resisting temptations—they end up locked in a battle with the very thought they are trying to avoid.

Carl Jung, the founder of analytical psychology, once said: "What you resist, persists. What you accept, transforms."

When you try to resist temptation, you actually intensify the impulse you're trying to suppress—whether it's eating that old vanilla ice cream that's been sitting in the freezer for six months instead of packing your gym bag; crashing on the couch after work instead of going for a jog; turning on the TV after dinner instead of meal prepping for tomorrow; or scrolling through Instagram instead of writing in your journal.

Suppressing thoughts, urges, and cravings makes them feel even more captivating and compelling because your brain presumes that your thoughts are crucial information providers. When a suppressed thought keeps coming back—thanks to the automatic mind checking that you're not thinking about it—your brain concludes that it must contain important information that needs your attention.

So, if thought suppression doesn't work, how do you fight temptations?

The solution lies in accepting that you have the urge—you feel the temptation. You can even say it out loud without judging yourself: "I feel that resistance. I don't want to prep food for tomorrow. I want to watch TV instead."

Accept the feeling, even if it's a little uncomfortable, instead of trying to suppress it. Over time, you'll notice that uncomfortable feelings last just a couple of minutes. You don't need to react to the feeling —just accept it without judgment. Hear yourself. You can still watch TV after you do your meal prep. Then, take action for just two minutes. **Quickly finish** prepping meals for tomorrow, and then turn on the TV.

ONE DAY AT A TIME VS. IRONIC REBOUND

Here's a hack: use the concept of "one day at a time" when eating healthily and moving your body in a loving manner. The "one day at a time" mindset has allowed severely addicted people to stay clean, sober, and keep their addictions in check for years.

Whether it's alcohol, cigarettes, sugar, or other addictive substances, when people realize they're supposed to stay away from them forever, ironic rebound starts sabotaging their efforts. "You shall never eat sugar [drink beer, smoke cigarettes, insert your favorite poison here], ever again!" suddenly sounds like a death sentence.

Now, consider this instead: *Instead of eating a donut for breakfast, I will have delicious scrambled eggs with my favorite toppings.* Doesn't it feel easier to imagine enjoying a good, healthy breakfast, lunch, and dinner just for today, without fixating on a sugar-free eternity?

I want you to focus on eating well and moving your body just for today, or even for the next hour to calm your limbic system down. Don't think of tomorrow, a week from now or an upcoming event next summer. Focusing on today feels much more doable and can help to stay on track.

BEST-CASE SCENARIO

Here's what you might experience when you start acting on your implementation intentions: You planned to eat more whole foods, go to the gym three times a week, and meditate daily. And for a couple of weeks or the next three days, you do your best to implement your intentions. Then something gets in the way—you skip your training session to sit on the couch, eat the same old way you always have, order a pizza one night, or forget to meditate. You realize that you've sabotaged yourself or put someone else's needs ahead of your own, and now you feel awful and too exhausted to change anything.

What can you do to prevent self-sabotage from pulling you off course and ensure these situations don't repeat? Once you make a mistake, hold your judgment and blame and instead use the experience as an opportunity to write your Best-Case Scenario.

In the ordinary course of life, people often feel overwhelmed, stressed, exhausted, angry, or lonely—sometimes all of the above. They count on their willpower to push through self-sabotage, which shows up as procrastination (hello, social media), perfectionism (*I ate pizza for dinner, might as well continue eating all the food*), or people-pleasing (*I had to take that extra work*). The willpower battery is often drained, which is why relying on other tools for support can help them stay the course.

It would be ideal, but you cannot expect that you will never be tempted to skip the gym, eat highly processed food, or miss meal prep. So instead of just hoping for the best-case scenario, write it. Develop a detailed and specific plan to combat decision fatigue before it escalates into full-blown self-sabotage. This way, you won't need to rely on willpower to make the best decisions—you'll be prepared to execute your plan and knock down resistance before it even starts.

The best time to engage your prefrontal cortex's decision-making power and design a best-case scenario for what your actions will be when you are triggered is when your willpower is strong. This way, you don't have to make a choice about what to do—you will simply follow your own instructions. Your self-sabotage is most likely following a habit structure: cue, routine, reward. The cue triggers a set of actions to get the "usual" reward for the tired brain.

The objective of your best-case scenario is to override one of your old habit structures. Find your cue, change the routine, and upgrade the reward.

Sandra decided to hit the gym on Monday, Wednesday, and Friday on her way home from work. But she noticed a pattern of missing the gym's exit on autopilot and continuing to drive home. She only realized she had missed the gym when she got out of the car and saw her unused gym bag.

Last time this happened, Sandra got really disappointed, crashed on the couch with a bowl of salty snacks, and felt unable to do anything else. Her cue trigger for this habit structure was a certain time of day—5 p.m.—and a combination of specific situations and feelings. Sandra felt tired and hungry after work and successfully drove home five days a week. She "forgot" to go to the gym because she felt too tired to work out and too hungry to wait for dinner afterward.

Her habit routine was the luxury of lying on the couch with snacks after a busy workday. The reward her brain looked forward to was the feeling of rest. For Sandra's brain, the act of skipping the gym and eating salty "treats" felt like self-care.

After looking closely at the cue, routine, and reward, Sandra decided that her best-case scenario to actually exercise at the gym three days a week was to do a short meditation and get a smoothie at the gym before changing into her workout clothes.

Sandra's cue stayed the same—feeling tired and hungry after work. But instead of enduring hunger and forcing herself to work out on an empty stomach, she recharged her energy with a delicious and nutritious smoothie and a short guided meditation in the gym's rest area. The smoothie stabilized her blood sugar, gave her energy for the workout, and helped her fight cravings. The guided meditation gave her tired brain a much-needed rest before the workout.

Now, when Sandra hits the couch after dinner, wearing her cozy PJs, watching her favorite show with a delicious cup of herbal tea, the reward her brain gets is even sweeter. Instead of feeling guilty for skipping the gym and eating junk, she feels proud for keeping her word to herself, energized by her workout, and nourished by her healthy food. Her salty snacks no longer call her name because she has given her brain the reward it used to seek. She experiences zero cravings because all of her senses are completely satisfied. The rest on the couch feels even greater and well-deserved.

When you make a mistake, rejoice—now you get to create a best-case scenario to make sure it won't happen again. Use the Best-Case Scenario Template to help.

To access the
Best-Case Scenario Template

SCAN THE QR CODE:

SCAN ME

DARE

"I am a lover of what is, not because I'm a spiritual person,
but because it hurts when I argue with reality."
– Byron Katie, American author and speaker

I want to share a tool that helps me respond instead of react.

When people feel stressed, their usual reaction is to avoid it, numb it, or pull others into their experience. Stress can lead to self-sabotage in the form of emotional eating, procrastination, numbing out with social media and TV, or yelling at people.

This tool helps you respond deliberately by choosing a behavior that will bring a more desirable outcome instead of reacting on autopilot.

I find that, as a society, we have made huge progress in emotional intelligence. When I was growing up, we never discussed emotions. The general attitude from teachers in my kindergarten was "Shut up and listen." My daughter, however, was taught to recognize her emotions and regulate them. I mean, if you want to avoid eating your emotions, this is exactly what you need.

When you are reviewing your day and have a nagging feeling because you were drawn into an automatic reaction and snapped at your partner, just dive into an investigation process I call DARE. **DARE** is an abbreviation of **Describe, Accept, Review,** and **Exceed**, making it easy to remember when you need to amend a behavior you are not proud of. These actions allow you to make peace with your feelings, address the root cause, and find a better solution.

I have to remind you to refrain from beating yourself up and replace judgment with curiosity. This way, you can avoid an automatic reaction such as trying to numb or run away from feelings of guilt and shame.

I invite you to dive in...

Describe It: Whatever happened, happened. Breathe. Get out of autopilot by staying in the present moment and remember what you were feeling before the behavior manifested itself. Feelings are indicators of our vibration, the energy state we are in. Describe the feeling. You can also use the List of Feelings I share with you to better understand it. The List of Feelings helped me recognize and name what I was feeling at the beginning of my own journey into emotional intelligence.

To access the
List of Feelings

SCAN THE QR CODE:

SCAN ME

Describe it example: Martha yelled at her husband when they were about to leave for a fun family outing at the zoo.

I wanted to yell.

Why?

I didn't want him to rush me.

Why?

I was feeling too overwhelmed. I was busy answering my work emails and felt tired because I had to wake up too early to get ready for the outing.

Accept It: You don't have to love the feeling. Just like the weather—you don't have to love the rain. Acceptance is just letting it be. Your feeling exists, so don't deny, suppress, or avoid it. The same way you don't pretend it's not raining, don't pretend you're not feeling something. At the same time, don't succumb to self-pity. Your brain will try to skip painful feelings by pulling attention elsewhere, such as to your bruised ego. But the feelings will keep coming back until you accept them. When you allow yourself to fully feel the discomfort, it takes less time for it to pass.

Researchers found that the intense part of a feeling lasts for about a minute and a half.

Don't attach judgment to the feeling, and let go of trying to control the situation. It is what it is. The situation will only change for the better when you stop trying to control it, stop reacting to it, and start responding in the best possible way. If you try to change the situation while still in reactive mode, you will create more disappointment, resentment, and hurt.

In the book *Alcoholics Anonymous*, commonly known as the "Big Book," primarily written by Bill Wilson, notes: "Acceptance is the answer to all my problems. When I am disturbed, it is because I find some person, place, thing, or situation—some fact of my life—unacceptable to me. I can find no serenity until I accept that person, place, thing, or situation as being exactly as it is supposed to be at this moment..."

Review It:

Now that you have described the feeling and accepted it, you can go to the source of the feeling, the thoughts that create it. If you allow yourself to go deeper, you might also discover the beliefs that create those thoughts. Beliefs that you inherited or were created as a result of going through difficult situations. You might also find out that these beliefs are no longer helpful; they keep you at the old set point. Once you see that they are obsolete, you can stop regarding those beliefs as true, and the thoughts created by those beliefs stop resurfacing. Once you go through this exercise, you will be amazed to find yourself in the same situation and act constructively instead of falling into the old pattern. To **review it,** ask yourself:

- Which thought created this feeling?
- Which belief is behind it?

Exceed It: By "Exceed it," I mean to do better, and go beyond it in finding a more appropriate solution. Chances are the situation will repeat itself, but you can respond and create a more positive outcome instead of reacting. In Exceeding it you can decide on a more beneficial action that would get you through a similar situation feeling proud of how you handled it instead of wasting your energy on regrets and shame. You can ask the following questions to find out which actions will help you **exceed it:**

- Which action would be a more positive response to the feeling?
- Which action will directly address the needs of your body, mind, or soul?
- Do you need to feel connected?
- Do you need to reset with a meditation, walk or a nap?
- Are you craving more support?

By addressing your real needs in these situations, you can stop falling into compulsive behavior. In Martha's example, she snapped at her husband when she felt overwhelmed. The driving thoughts behind feeling overwhelmed were: *We are late. We won't have time to see all the animals in the zoo. Children will be disappointed. I am a bad mother.* The belief that created those thoughts was: *When a woman has a career, her family will suffer.* Martha made a conscious decision that she was allowing herself to have it all and enjoy her life. She even created an affirmation to help her counteract that belief: *I have all the time in the world for my work and my family.* She established that in case the feeling of overwhelm arises the next time she's getting ready to leave with her family for an outing, she would take three deep breaths and ask her husband to take over a couple of her tasks.

GETTING FAMILY AND FRIENDS TO PARTICIPATE IN YOUR HEALTHY LIFESTYLE

Whether you want it or not, people around you will be touched by the changes you are making in your lifestyle. If you are quitting smoking, some people around you might be upset to lose their smoking buddy. If you quit drinking, you will disrupt the routine of the people you went out with. Some people might feel threatened by your new diet, fearing that they will have to stop eating ice cream in front of you to avoid tempting you. And they might have a point. The way you approach your lifestyle and your tribe might endanger your commitment or facilitate your success on the way to your goal.

If you prepare yourself in advance before discussing your healthy lifestyle with your loved ones, you can ensure that everyone feels heard, loved, and appreciated, making your transformation smoother.

I have some tips that can help turn a sensitive conversation into a supportive one—or, at the very least, avoid pushback.

First of all, don't seek advice from people who have never succeeded in what you are planning to do, and don't share your big goal with people who have never achieved anything similar. Their reactions are shaped by their life experiences and awareness. I believe your loved ones have good intentions, but if they have never achieved the success you are aiming for, they might not see your vision or fully understand what you are trying to do.

If you are an adult, don't ask for permission to live your life the way you want. Instead, ask for support.

It is very helpful to explain exactly what you are doing. Your loved ones' brains work the same way as yours; they appreciate clarity and knowing what's next. When people lack information, their minds tend to imagine the worst, leading to negative reactions.

For example, when Leslie told her partner she was going on a diet without explaining what that meant, he assumed they would eat nothing but poached chicken breast and spinach from then on. Upset by the idea, he even told her he wasn't going to give up popcorn when they watched movies. To him, their fun was over, and their life together was over. He feared that once Leslie lost weight, she would leave him because she could no longer love him.

When worst-case scenarios trigger fear, your loved ones might react negatively and seem unsupportive of your decisions.

You can avoid confrontation and rising tension by clearly explaining the changes you're making, which shared activities will remain the same, and how much you still value your time together. Show and express appreciation for them in your life. It's also worth mentioning how important these changes are to you and how much their support would mean.

Encourage them to share their concerns and ask questions about what you've just shared. Have a discussion about how you can handle any challenges together.

Maybe they'll even want to be part of your success story—help cook a meal or two, try a new recipe, or meal prep together on the weekend.

You might need to ask them to help you avoid foods you tend to overeat or that trigger unhealthy habits. You might also need their support in refraining from certain comments like, "You don't need to waste your time and money learning which foods suit your body chemistry. You don't need to lose weight. You're just built this way. We're naturally on the heavier side." Your loved ones likely mean well, but they may not be aware of how lifestyle choices influence genetic expression. You don't have to explain epigenetics—just wait until they see your results and are ready to understand why it works.

LIVE AND LET LIVE

Sometimes, even after having an honest and open discussion, your loved ones may remain unsupportive. They may not share your awareness or want to take part in your transformation—and that's okay. Everyone is on their own journey, with their own Higher Power guiding them. They will find their own way.

There are countless roads leading to the same destination—to the highest universal good. Your loved ones' path to happiness might look different from yours. They may never adopt your healthy lifestyle or share your values, but they will reach their own understanding of what is best for them in their own time.

Lead by example, love them unconditionally, and choose to see the best in them.

Training yourself to see the best in all people is the next level of personal growth. See them with your new awareness, and help them appreciate themselves. This exercise mirrors the good that exists within you.

If you find that people around you feel threatened by your new lifestyle to the point of sabotaging you, you may need to set boundaries and firmly protect them by being assertive. In this case, the assertiveness formula is the best way to communicate how you feel, what you want people to stop doing, and what you want them to do instead.

Here's the formula:

WHEN YOU DO → I FEEL → I NEED YOU TO STOP → AND DO INSTEAD

For example, when Darlene decided to stop drinking alcohol, her boyfriend continued to buy her favorite wine and serve it with dinner. Darlene felt betrayed and angry, and she wanted to punish him by leaving. After consulting with her counselor, she decided to use the assertiveness formula. She remained calm, took three deep breaths, and said:

"When you serve me my favorite wine, I feel tempted and upset because I am trying really hard to avoid it. I need you to stop buying alcohol for me and serving it at dinner. Instead, please buy me mineral water as my drink for dinner. You can continue drinking alcohol in front of me—I appreciate your support."

After Darlene explained to her boyfriend what she needed, he started serving her mineral water instead. She didn't need to leave him, nor did she need to scream to be heard. She simply needed to explain which specific action was triggering her feelings and what she wanted him to do instead.

When setting boundaries, be specific about the action that triggers a feeling in you and avoid blaming the person's character.

THEY CAN'T MAKE YOU FEEL ANYTHING—UNLESS YOU ALLOW IT

Part of maintaining strong boundaries is taking responsibility for your thoughts, feelings, actions, and results. Other people have the right to their opinions and actions, and their opinions don't have to disrupt your choices—unless you allow them to.

At its core, what others think about you depends on their beliefs and values. You don't have to take their opinions to heart. When you allow yourself to be affected by what others say, you lose your freedom and imprison yourself.

The need to be liked by everyone—also known as people-pleasing—is another form of self-sabotage. When you need support, don't rely on the approval of others—rely on a Power Greater Than Yourself, rely on unconditional love. This force is incredibly powerful. Those who anchor themselves in unconditional love don't live in fear, aren't easily distracted by external circumstances, and trust that when they do their best, life will unfold in their favor. They live in complete freedom.

People might judge you when they hear, for the first time, that you have decided to spend time doing what you love. They might even call you selfish or unhelpful. Let go of their judgments. Their reactions reflect their own conditioning, not your truth.

You only get one life. You can live it trying to please everyone around you, or you can live it for yourself and those you truly love. You can't do both—it's exhausting. You must choose what to prioritize. You are essential.

Ask for help, delegate, and be willing to receive help. I don't know which is harder—asking for help or accepting it—but both are part of becoming the best version of yourself. Just ask, and resources and support will come through the people around you. The Universe will provide. We were never meant to do everything alone. Traditionally, people lived in large communities and families. Even five-year-olds had responsibilities. Organizing your household and delegating tasks are skills you can develop over time.

If you think that asking for help burdens your loved ones, just know that continuing to do everything yourself will be a greater burden in the long run. I must warn you—if you keep handling everything alone, you will eventually burn out. That's why I included monitoring your mental state in the Planning–Monitoring for Success Worksheet.

I am convinced that my mother's story would have been completely different—and that she would still be alive—if she had made self-care a priority and accepted help. She lived in a state of burnout for years while battling cancer. There is growing evidence of how a person's mental state affects physical health. Disease is the absence of ease in the body. Engaging in feel-good activities regularly can help you live a happier and longer life.

Your lifestyle affects your energy, and your energy affects the people around you—it's a ripple effect you cannot avoid. The way you treat yourself shows others how you expect to be treated. If you have children, they will model your lifestyle because you are setting an example.

There is no way to tiptoe through life without making an impact on others. Everyone serves as either a great example or a terrible warning. You get to choose which one you want to be.

Think about ways to get your loved ones involved in what you're doing so that your new lifestyle is sustainable. Cooking separate meals for yourself is not manageable in the long run. You can turn it into a family activity: sit down together to find the healthiest versions of your favorite recipes, plan and prepare meals as a team, and get excited about trying new foods or recipes. This will benefit everyone. Your loved ones can also learn how to cook, so when you're too busy, they can step in.

The more you enjoy daily tasks together, the better the energy in your home will be, and the smoother your journey toward your goal will become.

WHEN YOU ASK FOR HELP, EXPLAIN EXACTLY WHAT YOU NEED AND WHAT YOU DON'T NEED

Better communication with those around you can prevent many unnecessary disruptions. Most people don't clearly express what they need, assuming that what they are asking for is common knowledge.

However, assumptions are not based on facts—they are based on illusions.

If you assume your partner knows exactly what you want and expect them to do it your way, you are setting yourself up for disappointment and unnecessary drama.

Here's an example of an assumption-based disappointment: when Susan asked her husband to watch their baby while she was away for the day, she expected to return home to a smiling father bonding with their happy daughter, a tidy house, and a ready-to-eat dinner—because that's what she usually did when she was home with the baby. She bonded with her while cooking dinner, and then they had a fun game to put the toys away. That night, however, she came home to an exhausted father, a cranky child, and a house that looked like it needed a cleaning crew of ten.

"What happened? You didn't put the toys away? You didn't cook dinner?" Susan asked.

"What did you expect? I was watching the baby all day!" her husband replied.

Your loved ones want to support you and be as helpful as possible, but they don't always know which specific actions would actually help. If they guess, you might not like the result. It is your responsibility to ask for help and to communicate exactly what you need.

By doing so, you can prevent friction. Imagine a world where communication is so clear that you fully understand your loved ones, and they fully understand you. Most family conflicts arise from simple misunderstandings—misinterpretations of what was said and what was interpreted. Every aspect of life that involves other people, including your intimate relationships, can be improved by clearly communicating your needs. But remember: *you must first know what you want in order to communicate it effectively.*

KEY POINTS

1. Change your environment to avoid temptations rather than fight temptations.
2. Discount your temptations by delay.
3. Adapt your environment to your new self-image.

4. Suit Up & Show Up for Two Minutes.
5. Find your way to do annoying but necessary daily tasks for your well-being.
6. Use One Day at a Time vs. Ironic Rebound.
7. Create a Best-Case Scenario.
8. Use DARE to prevent relapsing into unwanted behavior.
9. Getting family and friends to participate in your healthy lifestyle.
10. Live and let live.
11. They can't make you feel anything—unless you allow it.
12. When you ask for help, explain exactly what you need.

CONCLUSION
WHAT'S NEXT?

I hope you've learned some tips from this book that can help you reach the next level of becoming the best version of yourself, creating a low-effort healthy lifestyle, and feeling and looking great.

I use the **Hollywood Body Method** to help my clients implement lifestyle changes. The method helped me to transform my body and the bodies of my clients by creating a goal that ignites, then designing a new self-image, discarding old layers of self-sabotage, living the best life from the new self-image, and falling in love with the new self. As with actors, preparation, technique, and any external changes start with internal work.

These are **the FOUR PILLARS** for achieving your optimal well-being goal that I laid out in this book: **Setting a Goal** and **Creating a New Self-Image, Removing the Old Self-Image, Acting from the New Self-Image, and Manifesting Evidence of the New Self-Image.**

When you go through the four pillars, I suggest using the following checklist to see your progress. And I want to remind you that you don't have to do everything overnight. Use the Hollywood Body Method to gradually implement new actions. The Japanese call this Kaizen—a 1% improvement every day. This will enable you to implement a healthy lifestyle with low effort. There's no shame in making it easy. When your brain perceives it as easy, your journey becomes effortless, and you can actually stick to the new actions.

CHECKLIST

When using this checklist, you must be able to check off each item before moving on to the next.

NEW HABITS:

- I have a clear and detailed goal and vision of what success looks like, and I spend at least a couple of minutes each day imagining myself already embodying that person.
- I have a lucky charm to keep me connected to my goal and bigger vision.
- I have a detailed plan for foundational, dopamine, and feel-good actions that take up 10% of my waking hours each week.
- I review my day, week, and month to draw conclusions and improve rather than beating myself up.
- I monitor my mental health to avoid burnout.
- I have a solid morning routine that I follow every day (or most days), which starts my day from a peak state, a place of awareness and intention.
- I actively work on allowing uncomfortable feelings rather than numbing or avoiding them, and I release judgments.
- I take my feel-good activities seriously and engage in regular self-care practices that help me feel more connected—body, mind, and soul, as well as to something greater than myself.
- I take steps to battle Self-Sabotage by becoming aware of it, reflecting on what my future will look like if I don't override it, and considering the best-case scenario.
- I use the Suit Up and Show Up for Two Minutes code to fight resistance.

OLD HABITS:

- I've completed my Habit Structure Worksheet for the habit I want to change (identified my cue, the routine, and the reward I'm getting) and have chosen a specific new routine to replace it while still achieving a similar reward.
- I have a clear best-case scenario for what to do in this situation. If this is a behavior I regularly struggle with (either avoiding something I should be doing or doing something I shouldn't be doing), I have made a detailed plan for exactly what I will do the next time I find myself in this situation.
- I replace judgment with curiosity and follow the DARE steps (Describe it, Allow it, Review it, Exceed it) to work through the feelings and thoughts driving this behavior.
- I conduct a Behavior Review and challenge the unhelpful thoughts fueling my feelings and actions.
- I use delay to discount, taking advantage of the brain's natural tendency to be less interested in rewards that are far away in time or distance.
- I change perception by considering the immediate and long-term negative implications of engaging in this behavior.

HABITS FOR LONGEVITY

Consistency in a healthy lifestyle is the key to living longer, looking better, and feeling amazing. These habits helped me lose weight and keep it off:

- Habit #1: Eat when hungry.
- Habit #2: Eat till 80% full.
- Habit #3: Use the anti-perfectionism rule: when you eat 90-80% of whole, natural, good-quality food and allow up to 20% processed food, it's a great progress. If you eat too much or too much processed food, don't shame or punish yourself. Instead just make the next meal as balanced and as natural as possible.
- Habit #4: Drink enough water on an empty stomach.

- Habit #5: Plan and prep healthy food: balanced meals, containing whole, natural, good quality seasonal food.
- Habit #6: Make it hard to eat processed foods.
- Habit #7: Make it easy to eat healthy.
- Habit #8: Daily movement and exercise.
- Habit #9: Be your biggest fan; don't allow self-criticism to surface.
- Habit #10 Use Planning–Monitoring for Success Worksheets to plan your actions, monitor your success, your energy, to make time for daily feel-good activities, and to correct your actions to reach your goal faster.

WHAT'S NEXT?

This is what I learned after studying biology, anatomy, neuroscience, epigenetics, nutrition, naturopathy, etc.—unless people study these subjects, they don't know how to achieve their ultimate well-being. Unfortunately, we aren't given manuals on what to do exactly to keep our bodies healthy and in the best shape. Schools teach us some general information about the human body—more than in the past—but still not enough to understand what we need to do to feel our best.

So, when you think about losing **20–30 pounds** or **getting into shape** so you can wear your favorite pair of pants and love the way you look, what comes to mind? Eat less and exercise more, right? Maybe count calories, eat low-carb or high-protein, try intermittent fasting, or even become vegetarian?

You might try everything—detoxes, supplements, injections, exercise boot camps, or hormone-balancing programs—believing that intense effort is the only way forward. But here's the truth most media outlets don't talk about: All of these methods can work, but they might not work for your body. Let me explain.

To lose 20–30 pounds and keep it off, you need to understand **your body chemistry** and create **a plan** tailored to you.

As you know, I have been a yo-yo dieter since I was 14. I wanted to lose 10 pounds but ended up gaining 20. I tried everything—low-carb diets, weight-loss pills, liposuction, two hours of cardio five days a week, calorie counting, and detoxes. You name it, I've done it.

I remember attempting a low-carb diet like so many others. By the third week of eggs, meat, salads, and occasional cheese, I was desperate for something sweet. Someone mentioned apple pie, and I found myself at the store, buying two Snickers bars. That binge caused me to gain 20 pounds in just one month. I truly understand why diets feel impossible.

I also tried detoxing. Once, I ate nothing and only drank liquids for three days. I counted the hours, weighed myself three times a day, and lost five pounds—only to gain back seven pounds three days later when I resumed "normal" eating. That experience taught me a crucial lesson: I simply **can't go for days without food**. Sorry, but I just can't.

Here's the secret nobody is telling you: **Nailing your body chemistry is the best way to lose 20 pounds and keep it off.**

A low-carb diet might be completely wrong for your body. A so-called "healthy" detox might contain ingredients that actually make you gain weight. If you follow a diet that isn't compatible with your unique body chemistry, it can lead to inflammation, water retention, and stalled weight loss.

Some people eat very little yet still gain weight because their bodies aren't processing food efficiently. The wrong diet can also deprive your body of essential nutrients, creating food noise—a constant mental obsession with food that leads most people to quit within weeks and gain even more weight.

This is why I don't recommend randomly trying diets. While some methods work for some people, they shouldn't be attempted without first understanding **your body chemistry**.

So, if diets don't work for everyone, detoxes can contain inflammatory foods, and supplements are often expensive and ineffective, what's the best option for busy professionals with active family lives who don't want to spend hours at the gym? :)

I'm so glad you asked! And I'm super excited about this strategy. The answer is (drum roll): build a **Forever Young Protocol**™.

But what exactly is the Forever Young Protocol™? It's a **personalized nutrition and longevity strategy** designed to align with your body chemistry. This approach helps you balance hormones, reduce cravings and stress, optimize sleep, strengthen your immune system, and so much more. Along with expert guidance, you'll receive three meal plans tailored **to the foods you enjoy,** a structured strategy to help you **live longer, look younger, and feel happier,** plus plenty of support from me.

WHY BUILD THE FOREVER YOUNG PROTOCOL™ FIRST?

Because **we need to ensure that your meal plan and exercise program are compatible with your body chemistry.** Exercising too intensely can actually increase inflammation, making it harder for your body to release excess weight. That's why it's essential to focus on exercises that lower stress hormones and foods that truly work for your metabolism.

This realization was my big breakthrough after years of trying every weight-loss strategy. The most beautiful part? This method is straightforward, science-based, **and will save you time and effort** while delivering sustainable results.

For centuries, different traditions have attempted to personalize nutrition. Ayurveda classifies people through doshas, while traditional Chinese medicine uses the five elements. These systems recognize that different individuals require different foods and lifestyle adjustments to thrive. This concept also led to the classification of ectomorph, mesomorph, and endomorph body types and the development of metabolic-type diets.

However, the challenge with these highly respected methods is their lack of precision. Your metabolic needs change over time, requiring retesting every six months to recalibrate your approach. But why rely on guesswork when modern science offers a more precise solution?

By taking a DNA test, you can uncover your unique body chemistry once and for all. Unlike metabolic assessments that change over time, your genetic blueprint never changes—it's a one-time test that reveals your genetic strengths and weaknesses. By analyzing how your metabolic genes interact, we can create a detailed, personalized strategy to optimize your well-being.

Once you understand your genetic makeup, you can actively influence how your genes express themselves through lifestyle and nutrition. You can activate genes that promote vitality while minimizing the effects of genes that increase the risk of sickness. This is the key to achieving long-term weight loss, sustained energy, and overall well-being.

Here's the exact process to optimize your health:

1. Implement the right meal and exercise plan for your body chemistry to **speed up your metabolism**.
2. Optimize sleep, balance hormones, and regulate neurotransmitters to **eliminate cravings**.
3. Enhance detox pathways to **look 10 years younger and feel** incredible.
4. Create a low-effort healthy lifestyle to maintain long-term **well-being**.

That's it! It sounds simple, right? But in reality, it took me years to perfect this system.

Several crucial factors affect your well-being that I would love you to become familiar with.

1. How to determine what foods work for your body chemistry to lose weight naturally.

There are many incredible doctors, nutritionists, and personal trainers who develop great programs, write books, and design diets to help people eat well and exercise effectively. From low-carb and high-protein diets to carb-loading and intermittent fasting, every approach has the potential to work—but only if it aligns with your unique body chemistry.

Unfortunately, most people are overloaded with conflicting information from the media. They end up trying everything at once—intermittent fasting, high-protein/high-fat diets, carb cycling, vegetarianism, high-intensity interval training, heavy weightlifting, sauna therapy, cold plunges, and a long list of supplements.

But here's the problem: If you're doing all of this, it's too much. You don't need every strategy—only the ones that specifically benefit your body.

Maybe you've followed certain programs before and achieved some results, only to lose motivation or feel drained, depressed, or overwhelmed. If you "fell off the wagon" early, midway, or even after completing a program, it's likely because the plan wasn't right for you.

Another major barrier to weight loss is food intolerances and inflammation. Allergies and intolerances can lead to leaky gut syndrome, triggering widespread inflammation that makes weight loss resistant. Identifying and eliminating foods that cause inflammation can significantly improve metabolism, digestion, and overall health.

Food intolerances contribute to poor digestion and affect metabolism. People who suffer from poor digestion cannot break down food and absorb the nutrients required to maintain effective metabolic function.

If digestion is compromised, the body struggles to burn calories and maintain a healthy weight.

To achieve lasting weight loss and overall well-being, you need a personalized approach. Generic diet plans might work temporarily, but they often fail in the long run. By understanding your body chemistry and making informed, science-backed choices, you can unlock sustainable health and vitality for life.

Inflammation can contribute to cravings and weight gain by affecting gut permeability. When partially digested food particles leak through the small intestine—where they don't belong—the immune system launches an attack, producing antibodies to combat these foreign invaders (antigens). This process triggers inflammation, which can lead to long-term health issues.

Many people unknowingly eat foods they are allergic to or intolerant to every day. As a result, their bodies continuously produce antibodies, forming immune complexes that contribute to joint pain, systemic inflammation, intense cravings, weight gain, and difficulty returning to a normal weight. However, because the inflammatory response to food allergies develops slowly, people often don't make the connection immediately.

People assume it's normal to experience heaviness after meals, bloating, gas in the afternoon, coffee cravings (especially with dairy), and occasional skin breakouts. But these are actually signals from the body that certain foods are causing distress. If left unaddressed, chronic exposure to the wrong foods can result in even more serious symptoms, including:

- Weight gain
- Fatigue
- Cravings
- Headaches, back pain, muscle pain, arthritis
- Mood swings, anxiety, depression
- Low libido
- Digestive problems (gas, bloating, diarrhea, constipation)
- Hormonal imbalances (PMS, irregular periods, menopause symptoms)
- Skin and hair issues (acne, hair loss, thinning hair, premature aging, facial hair growth in women)
- Frequent colds and infections

When people recognize these symptoms and attempt to improve their health with the wrong diet or exercise regimen, they may unknowingly increase inflammation and metabolic stress. This can lead to nutrient deficiencies, increased fatigue, food cravings, and a frustrating cycle where they feel worse instead of better.

People often fight cravings for as long as they can—until they snap. When this happens, they tend to give up, feeling discouraged, and take a break from their health journey. This cycle repeats because they are following generic diet and exercise advice that doesn't match their body chemistry.

If you feel tired, sluggish, and unmotivated, and you've decided it's time for a lifestyle change, it's essential to base your decisions on your body chemistry rather than one-size-fits-all health trends. The best way to achieve this is through scientific testing.

A DNA test can help you figure out which foods work for you and which don't. You can get answers about your lactose intolerance, as well as whether drinking coffee, matcha, green tea or peppermint tea or taking turmeric is beneficial for you. You can get answers regarding how much protein, fat, and carbohydrates your body requires daily. You can also get answers about vitamins and minerals your body is genetically deficient in. Your DNA test can show whether drinking raw cabbage juice or eating rucola is right for you or if it will do more harm than good.

Some people try really hard to follow the latest research discoveries by adding raw, vegan, or other biohacking superfoods, only to find out that they are feeling worse than before. They need to know if the superfood is actually compatible with their body chemistry.

And then, after you have an idea about what foods work best for your body, the next step is to create a meal plan consisting of the foods that are beneficial for your body chemistry with the right macros ratios that also please your taste buds and make you feel satisfied.

I am a foodie. I openly declare my love of food. I learned how to enjoy eating from my Italian friends when I lived in Florence. Food is one of the pleasures in life. And I firmly believe that feeling satisfied after a meal is important.

2. How to balance hormones to feel more energetic while you are getting in shape.

It's a very common issue: people often go overboard by drastically reducing calories while simultaneously adding muscle-building and intense cardio exercise programs. The problem is that without proper nutrition, blood sugar imbalances—combined with a hardcore workout routine—disrupt stress hormone production and the body's stress response. This throws off energy metabolism, hinders weight loss, prevents fat burning, and further destabilizes metabolic balance.

People start feeling drained, and they assume that it's normal to feel exhausted when they are trying to get in shape.

Not eating enough while attempting to adhere to a hard exercise program, in addition to modern-day chronic stress, generates additional stress hormones, disbalancing adrenals, dysregulating the hypothalamic-pituitary-adrenal (HPA) axis, and contributing to fat cell resistance.

The stress hormone's main function is to increase blood sugar levels so your brain and muscles have enough fuel to get you through a stressful situation. Many people don't feel hungry when faced with a stressful situation, but as soon as the acute stage of stress has passed, they feel ravenous hunger.

Stress activates fat storage that is four times as receptive in the abdominal wall. An extra layer of fat also serves as protection for the vital organs in the abdomen, because our body thinks that we are in danger. In a caveman's life danger was freezing temperatures *Must store more fat to survive.*

For many people, stress really impacts eating patterns and behaviors. People feel more tired and tend to have more cravings. Stress eating is a thing. This is one of the most common triggers for emotional eating. With stress, there is a tendency to eat more carbohydrates to keep energy up. Cravings for salty foods might also stem from the imbalances in stress hormones. Nobody can take away your stress, but I can help you optimize your genetic stress response to process stress without adverse effects on your well-being.

Getting in shape shouldn't feel exhausting. You need to eat enough to have energy for muscle building and for your daily tasks. Otherwise, it will be impossible to continue and to reach your goal. Your body needs to feel that it lives in abundance and safety to release the extra fat. That is why it is crucial to know how much protein, fat, and carbohydrates your body needs and also meet those requirements on a daily basis.

Knowing what type of exercise works best for your body can make your exercise sessions more effective. You might end up spending less time in the gym for your best shape. I also include a section on how to speed up your muscle recovery, avoid injury in the full report.

Besides stress hormones, low thyroid function might affect weight loss.

The thyroid regulates every cell in the body and sets the rate of the body's metabolic activity, body temperature, and thermogenic rate. Low energy, constipation, and depression are all symptoms of hypothyroidism, which can further contribute to weight gain.

Even subclinical hypothyroidism can affect energy expenditure. Research suggests that people with subclinical hypothyroidism can experience a metabolic slowdown up to 300-400 calories per day, which is fairly significant if we consider energy expenditure.

That is why I include the thyroid optimization suggestions in the DNA report.

Sex hormone imbalance influences your body composition.

An imbalance between estrogen and progesterone for women and estrogen and testosterone for men can have an impact on their body shape.

In women, progesterone is needed to equalize estrogen, and low levels can lead to estrogen dominance. Low progesterone can lead to bloating, water retention, weight gain, and puffiness.

Estrogen dominance can also contribute to an increase in thyroid hormone-binding globulin, which interferes with thyroid hormone activity. An imbalance between these two hormones can also affect insulin levels.

The DNA report clearly explains all major factors, including estrogen and testosterone, and provides recommendations on how to balance them.

3. How to optimize detox to look 10 years younger.

Your inflammation response and detoxification pathways affect your weight, skin, biological age, and your whole well-being. If your body struggles to eliminate toxins effectively, metabolic function will suffer.

A healthy liver is essential for weight loss. The liver is responsible for processing hormones, eliminating toxins, cleansing the blood, and breaking down fats. You can lighten your liver's load for a more effective function by reducing exposure to some chemicals that are linked to weight gain and obesity, so-called obesogens or endocrine disruptors. These chemicals can reprogram our stem cells in the body to produce more fat cells, and the effect of obesogens can be transferred to the next generation.

These are common chemical, dietary, pharmaceutical, and industrial compounds that can alter metabolic processes and predispose some people to gain weight. Avoiding these chemicals altogether is virtually impossible, but we can start by identifying them and choosing alternative products.

Some examples of endocrine-disrupting chemicals include BPA and PFAS, which are found in food storage containers, water bottles, certain non-stick cookware, and microwave popcorn bags. Parabens, commonly found in beauty products, have also been linked to weight gain. High fructose corn syrup—present in sodas, chocolate bars, fast food, and desserts—has shown obesogenic effects in animal studies. Artificial sweeteners have been associated with an increased risk of cardiovascular disease, kidney disease, and cancer.

For all of these reasons, I discuss how to reduce exposure to endocrine disruptors and include suggestions for enhancing detoxification, personalized based on your DNA report.

4. The role of sleep and movement is usually underestimated.

Sleep and diet are intricately linked. Studies show that a single sleepless night increases hunger and elevates ghrelin levels (the hormone responsible for appetite). Without adequate rest, people experience stronger cravings and slower metabolism.

Similarly, any form of movement is beneficial. Even after a short workout, the metabolic rate stays elevated for several hours, helping with long-term weight management.

5. Balanced neurotransmitter production is crucial to achieve your goals and feel great.

Dopamine and serotonin affect your mood and pleasure-seeking behavior, including cravings. You can balance these neurotransmitters naturally to feel amazing every day and control impulsive behavior. The recommendations for the neurotransmitter's genetic profile are included in the DNA report.

Most people follow unsustainable diets that they can't maintain long-term. They need a low-effort, healthy lifestyle that allows them **to live longer and feel happier**—without drastic restrictions.

This is why I am so passionate and excited to announce my Forever

Young Protocol™—a science-backed, personalized approach to achieving sustainable health, longevity, and weight loss. By aligning your diet, exercise, and lifestyle with your unique body chemistry, you can finally break free from ineffective health trends and create a lasting transformation.

I want to coach you to build a low-effort, sustainable, healthy lifestyle that you can consistently maintain using the framework I've developed. This exact process has helped me lose weight and keep it off for over twenty-five years.

I've also helped my clients lose 10, 20, even 70 pounds—with incredible success stories ranging from half a body weight lost in a year to a steady 10-pound loss in two months.

Is This You?

- You want to lose 10–20 pounds or more.
- You've been trying to do it on your own for a while (you're not a beginner) and want to stop the cycle of weight gain and keep the results.
- You want a low-effort healthy lifestyle to stay young and energized—without buying expensive supplements or injections.
- You strongly dislike restrictive diets (cutting carbs, eliminating fat, or following the latest "shiny new" strategy).

If this sounds like you, I'd love to have a conversation with you.

WHEN YOU COACH WITH ME, YOU GET:

- Meal plans, training, examples, masterclasses, checklists—the whole shebang!
- A framework trusted by Hollywood actors—it's your time to feel like a celebrity.
- Because I offer a personalized approach and work with each client individually, I have limited spots each month. Send me an email to info@irinacazazaeva.com to book a call when the next spot becomes available.

If you're unsure about the Forever Young Protocol™ because you don't want to eliminate your favorite foods—I've got your back. I'll make sure to include the foods you love in your meal plan so you can enjoy your journey.

If you think meal and exercise planning based on your body chemistry sounds complicated—I'll do it for you.

If you **don't want to spend hours prepping food**—no problem! You can order from a local supermarket or meal prep company. Meal prepping is NOT a requirement.

If you think that you have "fat genes," no worries. First of all, you can literally turn off the so-called "fat DNA." Once you understand your body chemistry, you can choose which genes get activated through your lifestyle and nutrition choices. The problem isn't your body chemistry—it's almost always the wrong food, the wrong exercise, and the wrong lifestyle for your unique body.

I would love to help you. Let's make sure it is a **great fit for both of us**. Let me know:

- What is your health goal?
- How much of a priority is it for you to feel great right now?

I will personally get back to you.

Again, you have absolutely nothing to lose and everything to gain.

I'm looking forward to speaking with you!

REFERENCES

INTRODUCTION

1. Ashtary-Larky, D., Chanavati, M., Lamuchi-Deli, N., Payami, S. A., Alavi-Rad, S., Boustaninejad, M., Afrisham, R., Abbasnezhad, A., & Alipour, M. (2017). Rapid weight loss vs. slow weight loss: Which is more effective for body composition and metabolic risk factors? *International Journal of Endocrinology and Metabolism*, 15(3), e13249. https://doi.org/10.5812/ijem.13249

2. Phuong-Nguyen, K., McGee, S. L., Aston-Mourney, K., Mcneil, B. A., Mahmood, M. Q., & Rivera, L. R. (2024). Yoyo dieting, post-obesity weight loss, and their relationship with gut health. *MDPI*. https://www.mdpi.com

3. Elia, M. (1992). Organ and tissue contribution to metabolic rate. In Kinney, J. M., & Tucker, H. N. (Eds.), *Energy Metabolism: Tissue Determinants and Cellular Corollaries* (pp. 61–79). Raven Press.

CHAPTER 1

1. Earl Nightingale, How to Completely Change Your Life in 30 Seconds

2. University of Scranton. (2012). Study on New Year's resolutions. *Journal of Clinical Psychology*. Summary:https://www.psychologytoday.com/us/blog/the-happiness-project/200910/stop-expecting-change-your-habit-in-21-days

3. *Walter Bradford Cannon (1932) The Wisdom of the Body*

4. *Encyclopedia Britannica* (2025)

5. Maltz, M. (1960). *Psycho-Cybernetics*. Prentice-Hall.

CHAPTER 2

1. Hebb, D. O. (1949). *The Organization of Behavior: A Neuropsychological Theory*. New York: Wiley and Sons. https://www.ncbi.nlm.nih.gov/books/NBK554483/

2. Queensland Brain Institute. Limbic System. https://qbi.uq.edu.au/brain/brain-anatomy/limbic-system

3. Penn Medicine. (2020). How Willpower Works. https://www.pennmedicine.org/updates/blogs/health-and-wellness/2020/january/how-willpower-works

4. The acronym HALT (Hungry, Angry, Lonely, Tired), from Alcoholics Anonymous

5. Wood, W., Tam, L., & Witt, M. G. (2005). Changing circumstances, disrupting habits. *Journal of Personality and Social Psychology*

REFERENCES

6. Lally P, van Jaarsveld CHM, Potts HWW, Wardle J. How are habits formed: modelling habit formation in the real world. Eur J Soc Psychol. 2010
7. Neal DT, Wood W, Labrecque JS, Lally P. How do habits guide behavior? Perceived and actual triggers of habits in daily life. J Exp Soc Psychol. 2012
8. Aniela Jaffé, Carl Jung, Memoirs, Dreams, Reflections, 1961
9. Wise, R. A. (2004). Dopamine, learning and motivation. *Nature Reviews Neuroscience*, 5(6), 483–494.
10. Terry Mullen, Letter to the St. Paul Pioneer Press, 1994
11. Hill, Napoleon (1937) *Think and Grow Rich*

CHAPTER 3

1. Bergmann, O., et al. (2009). Retrospective birth dating of cells in humans. *Cell*, 122(8), 1334–1348. https://www.cell.com/action/showPdf?pii=S0092-8674%2805%2900408-3

CHAPTER 4

1. Dusek, J. A., et al. (2008). Genomic counter-stress changes induced by the relaxation response. *PLOS ONE*, 3(7), e2579. https://doi.org/10.1371/journal.pone.0002579
2. Cameron, Julia, The artist's way, 1992
3. Maslow, Abraham, H, A theory of human motivation, 1943
4. Khan, H, A return to you, 2024

CHAPTER 5

1. Hicks, E. and J., Ask and it is given, 2004
2. *Psychology & Health*, 2018
3. Gollwitzer, P. M., & Sheeran, P. (2006). Implementation intentions and goal achievement: A meta-analysis of effects and processes. *Psychology & Health*, 34(2), 232–254. https://doi.org/10.1080/08870446.2018.1539487
4. Gollwitzer, P. M. (1993). Goal achievement: The role of intentions. *European Review of Social Psychology*, 4(1), 141–185. https://doi.org/10.1080/14792779343000059
5. Ruiz, D. M. (1997). *The Four Agreements*. Amber-Allen Publishing.
6. CPD UK. The Importance of Repetition in Learning. https://cpduk.co.uk/news/importance-of-repetition-in-learning
7. Gawain, S., Creative Visualization: Use the Power of Your Imagination to Create What You Want in Your Life, 1978

CHAPTER 6

1. Fromm, E., Man For Himself, 1947.
2. The Psychology Of Productivity, Psychology Today, 2024
3. Shearer, M. and M., The Charlotte Observer, 1986

REFERENCES

4. Voltaire, Dictionnaire Philosophique, Vol. 5., 1764
5. Goddard, N., The Power of Awareness, 1952

CHAPTER 7

1. Göllner, L. M., Ballhausen, N., Kliegel, M., Delay of gratification, delay discounting and their associations with age, episodic future thinking, and future time perspective, Psychology, 2018
2. Mischel, W., Study On Delayed Gratification, Stanford University, 1970.
3. Daniel Wegner, Thought Suppression experiments, 1987
4. Verduyn P, Delvaux E, Van Coillie H, Tuerlinckx F, Van Mechelen I, Predicting the duration of emotional experience: Two experience sampling studies. Emotion 9: 83–91. American Psychological Association, 2009, Vol. 9, No. 1, 83–91 1528-3542/09 DOI: 10.1037/a001461

CONCLUSION

1. Blumberg, B., & Loberg, K. (2018). *The Obesogen Effect.*
2. National Institute of Environmental Health Sciences. Bisphenol A (BPA). https://www.niehs.nih.gov/health/topics/agents/sya-bpa
3. Parabens and health. https://www.ncbi.nlm.nih.gov/pmc/articles/PMC9740922/
4. High Fructose Corn Syrup and obesity. https://www.ncbi.nlm.nih.gov/pmc/articles/PMC3522469/
5. Artificial sweeteners and cardiovascular risk. Harvard Health Publishing. https://www.health.harvard.edu/heart-health/sugar-substitutes-new-cardiovascular-concerns

THANK YOU FOR READING MY BOOK!

Just to say thanks for buying and reading my book, I would like to give you a free bonus gift, no strings attached!

Scan the QR Code:

I appreciate your interest in my book and value your feedback as it helps me improve future versions of this book. I would appreciate it if you could leave your invaluable review on Amazon.com with your feedback.
Thank you!

www.ingramcontent.com/pod-product-compliance
Lightning Source LLC
Chambersburg PA
CBHW021145090426
42740CB00008B/943